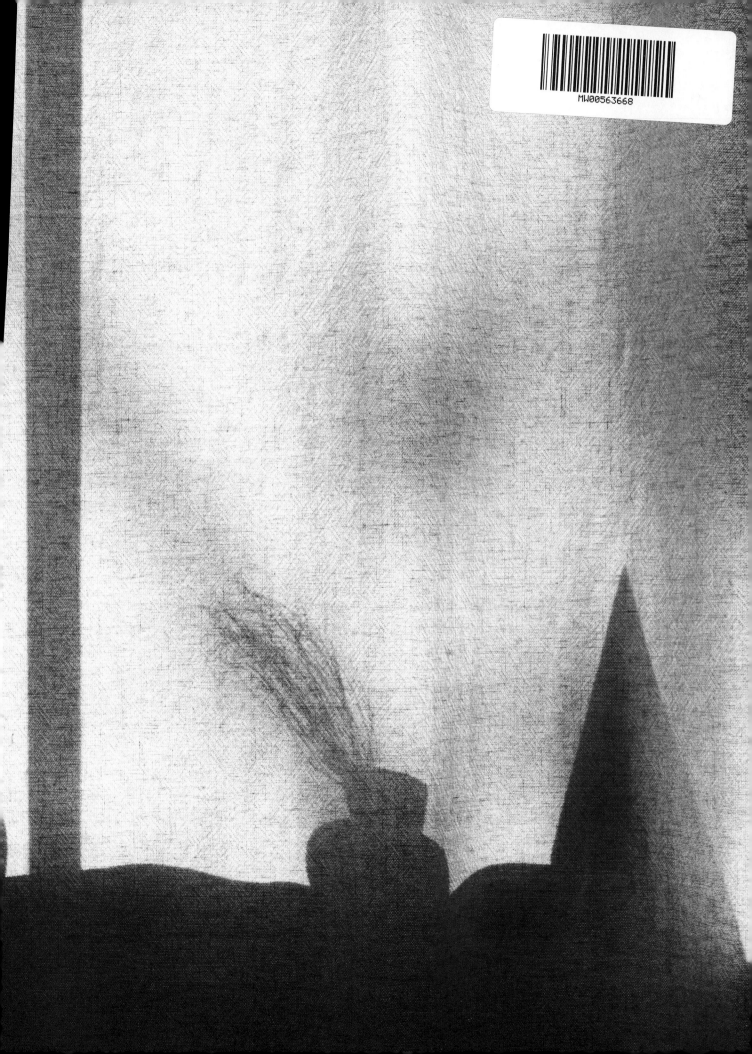

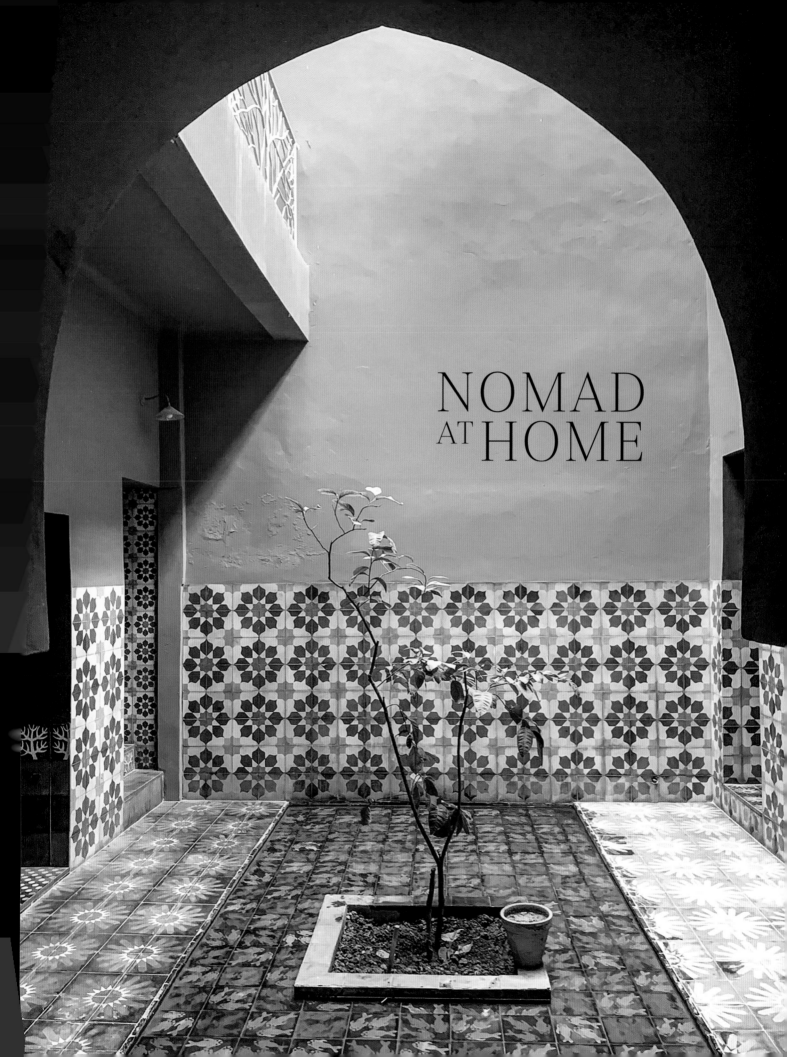

NOMAD
AT HOME

NOMAD AT HOME

Designing the home more traveled

HILARY ROBERTSON

FOREWORD BY LEANNE FORD

WITH PHOTOGRAPHY BY
MIKE KARLSSON LUNDGREN

RYLAND PETERS & SMALL
LONDON • NEW YORK

Design Paul Tilby
Senior commissioning editor Annabel Morgan
Production manager Gordana Simakovic
Creative director Leslie Harrington

For photography credits and copyright
information, see page 203.

Published in 2022 by Ryland Peters & Small
20–21 Jockey's Fields, London WC1R 4BW
and 341 E 116th Street, New York, NY 10029
www.rylandpeters.com

Text © Hilary Robertson 2022
Design © Ryland Peters & Small 2022
10 9 8 7 6 5 4 3 2 1
ISBN 978-1-78879-245-5

A CIP record for this book is available
from the British Library.

Library of Congress CIP data has been
applied for.

Printed and bound in China

FSC
www.fsc.org
MIX
Paper from
responsible sources
FSC® C008047

CONTENTS

For wanderers, drifters, gypsies, roamers, rovers, flâneurs, vagabonds... 8

The Borrowers 12

'Hotels like houses, houses like hotels'... 16

Local Gone Global 18

Materials Matter 24

Rooms with a View 32

Local Color – A Sense of Place 38

How to Nomad 48

THE WANDERERS 54

Anywhere But Here 56

Agnès in Wonderland 72

No Place Like Rome 84

Less is Moore 98

Nomadsland 112

Medina in Monochrome 126

Desert Hearts 142

Rock the Kasbah 158

Minimalists in the Medina 174

Hiraeth – A Longing for Home 186

Sources 202

Photography Credits 203

Index 204

Acknowledgments 208

FOREWORD

LEANNE FORD

I truly think Hilary Robertson is one of the greatest stylists, editors and curators of our time. (And don't even think about taking that line out, Hilary!)

I was reading Hilary's book *Monochrome Home* years before I even started thinking about a career in interior design – and I realized immediately that I had found my soul sister. Every page was bookmarked, every word was underlined, and everything had a Post-it note attached. I wanted to buy a second copy just so that I could rip out every page and hang them on my walls!

So I did what any super fan would do – I looked her up online. I found her on Instagram and sent her a quick message singing her praises from Pittsburgh. Her kind response truly made my day.

Years later, when my client Crate & Barrel asked me who I would like to bring in to style my first furniture campaign, I knew exactly who I wanted to call. That day I was so excited, and nervous, to meet the great Hilary Robertson herself. And now I am not only honored to work beside her and watch her brain work, I also have the joy of having my words in one of her wonderful creations – this book.

In Hilary I have found a kindred spirit. She is never afraid to play, to think bigger, to see what's out there and make it her own. She's a river of ideas: always inspiring, always intentional, and always pushing forward. She's never afraid to try new things, always excited to see new things, and, on a personal note, always showing me new things.

Hilary, thank you for putting your books out into the world. Thank you for your eye – for how you see the world, and for the gift of sharing with us what you see. I couldn't be more thrilled that we now have another book to dog-ear and underline. All I can ask is that you please keep going! Keep creating, keep traveling, and keep envisioning things more beautifully than most.

You're a true free spirit. The world needs more of those. So, THANK YOU. I am honored to be your friend.

XO, Leanne

FOR WANDERERS, DRIFTERS, GYPSIES, ROAMERS, ROVERS, FLÂNEURS, VAGABONDS...

Otherness has always attracted me. I would rather be a voyeur, an outsider rather than an insider; that's my default setting.

As a child, I identified the most seductive moment of my life as the night I tumbled out of a bunk bed on a Norwegian ferry in a storm. This was the climax of a voyage by sea on a stylishly designed ship where a three-year-old could spend hours in a state-of-the-art Scandinavian modern playroom, Scandinavians being characteristically more inclined to provide kindergarteners with interiors that are as thoughtfully designed as those for grown-ups. As this dramatic propulsion was the most unpredictable thing that had ever happened to me, I concluded (however subconsciously) that all journeys abroad were likely to provide excitement, a release from the banal and the ordinary course of life.

An addiction to travel was further encouraged with other trips; Amsterdam where the church bells rang through the night and the comforter was improbably large and fluffy like a cartoon cloud; France where my favorite camping site, situated in the grounds of a château, albeit a crumbling one, provided a stellar playground where an international crowd of junior campers could fight over the

monkey bars, a lake with inflatable orange dinghies, and my gastronomic highlight, piled-high bowls of straw-thin frites '*pour emporter*' available every evening from the château's kitchen (as middle class a Disney alternative as my parents could possibly dream up). Then there was Sweden where nudity in parks and sand dunes was normal and handfuls of pink shrimp were purchased, peeled, and eaten on the dock and all journeys started with a boat; or Jutland where, as a novelty, I would attend school in August (much ridiculed by the pupils for my Laura Ashley skirts and Victorian blouses) while my father worked.

After I had begun to learn languages, I was sent to summer with French and German exchange families to improve my conversational skills. Although not entirely pleasurable experiences (a strict French maman did not allow children to enter the kitchen, let alone plunder the refrigerator when hungry; an autocratic German father disapproved of New Romantic/Punk outfits, smudged kohl eyeliner combined with fishnets), I found myself asking where I might prefer to live one day, assuming I would have the choice. The problem of how I could escape the mundanity of my suburban home and swap the expected for the unexpected, the inherited for the exotic, was always my main preoccupation. My dolls lived in Paris. My shoes came from Copenhagen. My pencil case and satchel were always purchased in France before La Rentrée (the French term for September's back-to-school migration) as an end-of-summer treat.

Agnès Emery's rooftop salon, furnished with pomegranate-colored velvet benches, is open on one side but shaded by printed voile curtains.

Choosing another culture above your original one can be a complicated process. The initial seduction, the evolving fantasy about living in this 'other' place, the 'other' person you will become, grappling with realities: Can I speak the language? How can I work there? Where will I live? Who will my friends be?

There are few countries I have visited without consulting the local real estate agent's window or poring over the free property magazine. Because whether it's Puglia or Provence, I am already imagining my ideal life there; the basket I'll carry to market, the dress I might change into for an apéro in the square, the flea market at which I will buy my furniture, the secret cove where I'll swim, the clapped-out car I will buy from an ad in the post office, bar, local rag (I can't even drive). Thanks to Peter Mayle's memoir *A Year in Provence* and all the movies where downtrodden divorcées/workaholics are saved by slowing down, renovating a wreck, and producing small-batch olive oil/soap/wine/breeding llamas, the images are so familiar, the narrative predictable and yet still so desirable.

But as I have proven to myself, the course of nomadism doesn't always run smoothly and for the armchair fantasist, the realist, the pragmatist, there are other ways to achieve that feeling of global exoticism. The intrepid Design Nomad, whose taste for Moroccan rugs, Berber baskets, and tadelakt walls has been piqued by trips to the souk and sojourns at stylish riads run by French, Belgian, Dutch, and American expat adopters, can bring it all back home and set up their digs as an homage to the place for which they might almost leave home. Rather than break for the border, they can absorb the DNA and interpret the look just where they are. Creating Provence in Pittsburgh or Marrakech in Malmö can just as easily be achieved on the internet when you have evocative references collected on your Pinterest board, bookmarked sources in your virtual address book, and collaged the tear sheets onto your vision board.

Nomad at Home dissects the desire to wander from the point of view of the design-led traveler, both professional and amateur. It illustrates the stories of those who left home forever, those who managed to carve out lives in two, three, four countries, and also compulsive vacationers who found a way to bring their fantasy to life at home, just where they started; the armchair traveler whose deep research yields bookmarks bursting with design shops from Mallorca to Mexico City, whose exhaustive lists of restaurants and markets, beaches and bars are ready for the next journey, those for whom, in the words of Robert Louis Stevenson, 'To travel hopefully is a better thing than to arrive.'

An internal courtyard in Mexico is painted with elephant-gray limewash teamed with a faded red oxide on the lower third of the walls. These two-color combinations add decorative character, while the lime-based paint counters humidity.

THE BORROWERS

I am a self-confessed Borrower. The world is my dressing-up box. Other shops, other brands, other markets appeal to me so much more than the home-grown. Deciding to look outside my 'normal' setting for more exciting influences was a first step toward the metamorphosis from child into teenager. Like any self-respecting adolescent, I had to reject my mother's mini-me stylings: ladylike dresses, neatly coiffed hair, and patent-leather Mary Janes. I wasn't quite rebellious enough for a green Mohican and bondage pants, so oversized ruffled white shirts seemed a less controversial parent-friendly option – think Lord Byron or Adam Ant. I claimed my right to messy hair, a never-met-a-brush 'shag' (the late 1970s hairstyle that my mother assured me looked awful 'from the back'), a piratical rummage-sale ensemble loosely based on the New Romantics, and pointy suede Chelsea boots (I was too scared to enter Stephane Raynor's BOY but pressed my nose against the window to download the look). My makeover took me from tween to teen.

So naturally, when I am decorating my homes, from my university dorm room to my current digs in Brooklyn and CT, I turn my gaze toward somewhere else. And so ingrained is my addiction to visual escapism that I often rely on hotels to provide inspiration. Not any old hotel, of course, but places that I've discovered from friends, magazines, blogs, or just digging into a region or city on the internet: the classics like the Nord-Pinus in Arles, its rooms improved by a roster of notable bohemian visitors (Picasso, Cocteau et al) who left behind artworks, Amangiri in the Utah desert, an arrangement of buildings that blends modern architecture with an astonishing natural setting, or the trailblazers signaling a new mood and mindset like the Brutalist concrete Paradero in Todos Santos, Mexico or the minimalist Sublime Comporta in Portugal.

In Puglia, a contemporary chair by Slowood Studios is a timeless choice for the limestone-floored arched loggia (left). The chalky flatness of the shade of the warm gray walls is a foil for unruly greenery, a natural pairing of color and texture (opposite).

The interior designers and architects commissioned to dream up concepts for hotels, restaurants, and bars are often able to indulge in more extreme, fully fleshed-out themes and motifs than a domestic designer. Sometimes a limited budget can inspire material choices that are creative and unexpected, encouraging recycling or experimentation. If you are partial to hotel living or choose your Airbnb for the chance to experience a new aesthetic from the inside, you can learn many tricks from close examination of hotel design, from the furniture choices and arrangement of the room to the lighting. Hotels take comfort and durability seriously when developing an identity, so adapting design hacks from your last vacation is as valid an approach as any, and you get to 'try before you buy'. As the internet supersedes the high street as a shopping destination, hotels have a new role as showrooms for interior brands; I took a trip to Copenhagen's The Audo to sit on a sofa that wasn't

available to try out in NYC. The Soho House group has developed a range of interiors products, Soho Home, that you can purchase if you fall in love with the look of your room, and many other hotels have their own concept stores that allow you to buy into their 'lifestyle'.

Recent innovation in computer-generated imagery has produced extraordinary dreamscapes of places we might like to go, if only they existed. Instagram accounts such as @maison_de_sable, @visualpleasuretravel and @charlottetaylr are a rich seam of ideas for travel and design, taking existing locations, exaggerating and embellishing original structures and landscapes, and transforming them into nomad nirvanas where every trending trope is represented including arches, infinity pools, Brutalist terraces floating on water, desert oases, jungle cityscapes – concepts that inspire exploration both imaginary and visceral. Diving into Instagram to do some armchair design travel can trigger ideas to use wherever you land.

'HOTELS LIKE HOUSES, HOUSES LIKE HOTELS'...

(Sophie Hannah)

I love hotels. I can't get enough of them, while my husband loathes them, suspicious of the potential superficiality of the guest experience. As I'm always curious to experience all the ways in which good design can affect how I feel, I travel. Staying in another country gives me the opportunity to try out different atmospheres, design solutions, or recipes for living. Could I ever be a minimalist? Try the Morseta or Santa Clara 1728 in Portugal. Intrigued by the idea of living in a multihued maximalist fantasy? Head to El Fenn in the Marrakech medina. There's a hotel for every mood and design direction. When I plan a trip, I'm longing for an amplified feeling of wellbeing, a design hit that I can feel in my bones. That's what good architecture and design can do. It has to be worth leaving home for, but sometimes it shows you something you've missed about your own environment, something you can translate without resorting to pastiche.

An outdoor room has been created from very simple ingredients: a table made from terracotta pots supporting an old wooden door, a built-in banquette and rush stools provide seating (page 16). Ancient meets modern in a small town in Sweden where Lucas Morten has staged his neo- Brutalist pieces of furniture (this page).

LOCAL GONE GLOBAL

There's a global Mediterranean look that has been evolving over the past 20-plus years since Herbert Ypma identified the trend toward the smaller boutique hotel run by individuals not conglomerates in his series of *HIP Hotels* guides. The elements that combine to make this 'look' are not new or revolutionary in any way. Textural but spare, primitive but comfortable, this sort of rustic minimalism is defined by a pared-down, pragmatic mix of tried and tested local ingredients; walls in plaster, distemper, or limewash, timeless furniture, utilitarian textiles. These are rooms that are barely 'designed' at all; spaces that are unlikely to overwhelm the occupant with their distinctive personality, instead soothing them with unobtrusive comfort.

Taking style cues from boutique hotels, decorating with humbler, simpler materials – bamboo, rattan, seagrass, linen, clay – can work in many contexts beyond an exotic or bucolic setting. Casa Cook and The Rooster in Greece and Dorothée Meilichzon's Hotel Menorca Experimental have all developed an identifiable look that is catnip to a sophisticated traveler. It is essentialist by nature but relies on authentic qualities in the materials employed; a build-better, buy-better mindset. Furniture can be almost basic; think futon mattresses, plywood headboards, platform beds, and bench seating reminiscent of Valentine Schlegel, Robinson Crusoe-style four-posters made from bamboo poles or found timber, muslin canopies hung from the ceiling that are easy alternatives to more conventional bed frames. Denise Portmans ensures that her Airbnb guests sleep well by selecting durable wool mattresses combined with simple wooden box frames, and tufted handmade mattresses double as seating or daybed options both indoors and out at Masseria Potenti, Puglia when added to a painted wooden frame or concrete bench.

Riad Dar K reinterprets Moroccan
style in a modern way, embracing
textural but monochromatic style
(this page and opposite). Tadelakt
is used throughout for bathrooms,
floors, and walls. Yak-wool blankets
and woollen tassels decorate the
rough-hewn four-poster bed.

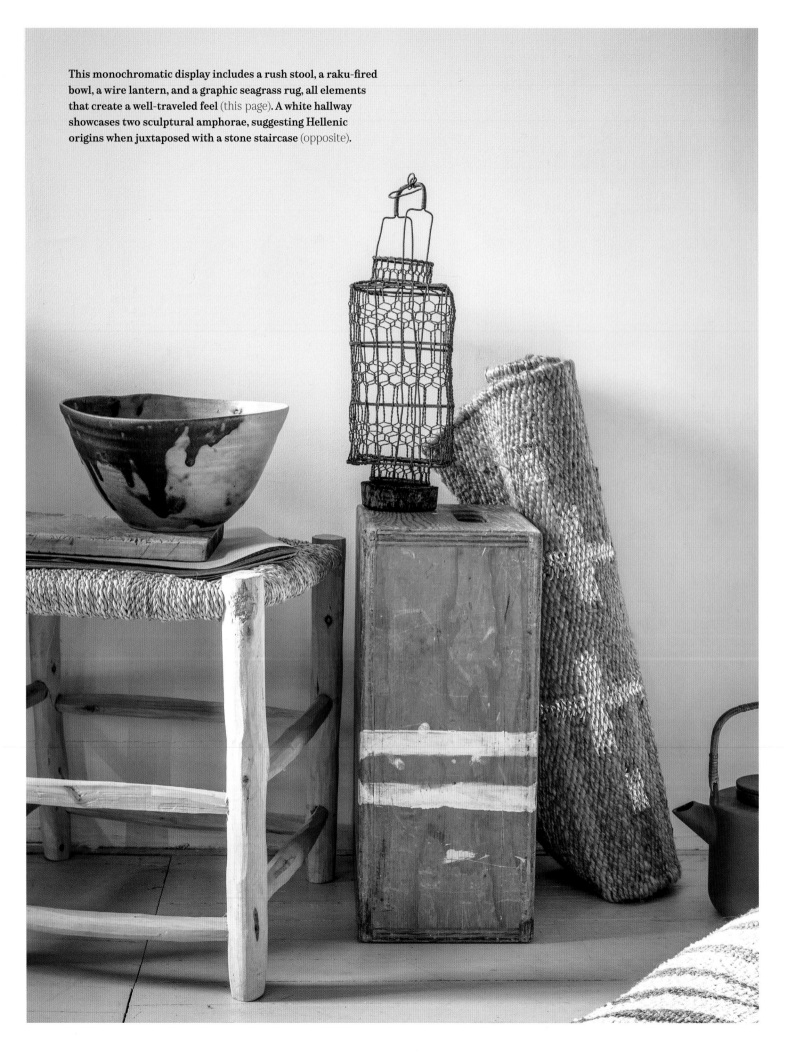

This monochromatic display includes a rush stool, a raku-fired bowl, a wire lantern, and a graphic seagrass rug, all elements that create a well-traveled feel (this page). A white hallway showcases two sculptural amphorae, suggesting Hellenic origins when juxtaposed with a stone staircase (opposite).

A materials still life brings
together elements for a
renovation: marble samples,
limestone, lava stone, and
pigments to mix into limewash.
Making a mood board from real
materials helps initiate ideas
for creating an atmosphere.

MATERIALS MATTER

It goes without saying that none of this simplicity would be as powerful or seductive if the right architectural 'envelope' did not exist for these humble ingredients.

Vernacular architecture, with its adobe, arches, roof beams, vaulted ceilings, brick, marble, or tadelakt floors, limestone details, and tiled walls, provides the building blocks of the nomad atmosphere: the rough stone walls at Casa Cook, the Cubist white-out of the San Giorgio hotel in Mykonos, the rough pinkish-brown of Berber Lodge's signature walls. And these textures, which give depth and character, can be 'borrowed' where appropriate for interiors in any location.

Instead of paint on drywall, try eco-friendly lime paint (with the right undercoat), or a traditional plaster or Roman clay; the reaction of daylight on tactile surfaces is more ethereal, revealing a depth and luminosity that paint cannot achieve. Don't underestimate the importance of the surface that you walk on both visually and sensually, either. Marble, stone, or tile are selected for their inherent 'coolness' in hot climates, whereas wooden floors suit the northern hemisphere better; both in context feel 'right' underfoot. Sensuous material choices make every room more agreeable to live in. The better the envelope of the room, the less you need to spend on the pieces you put in it.

Making a collection of large samples brings clarity for a renovation project. Seen here are slabs of Portuguese Estremoz marble, green serpentine stone, and limestone.

ON THE SURFACE
a glossary of tactile materials for
walls and floors

LIMEWASH
In Belgium, limewash or lime paint is the
go-to texture for walls, lending them the
modulated look of suede. Depth is achieved
with three or more coats. Made from slaked
lime mixed with water, it is colored with
natural pigments and it is a long-lasting
environmentally friendly alternative to paint.
On drywall, it requires an undercoat, a
mineral-based primer. If you are a fan of Axel
Vervoordt, this is the paint for you.

LIME PLASTER
A mixture of sand, slaked lime, and water,
lime plaster is permeable and breathable and
has a natural pH level that inhibits mold and
bacteria. Plastered walls have more depth and
modulation, qualities appealing to any fan of
wabi-sabi design.

ROMAN CLAY
This is a smooth gypsum-based finish applied
with a palette knife. The effect is similar
to Venetian plaster but more organic. It
can be sealed with wax and polished or left
unsanded for a low sheen appearance.

MILK PAINT
Milk paint is a VOC-free mixture of lime
and casein (milk protein). Like lime paint, it
works best on porous surfaces such as wood,
making it perfect for painted furniture,
doors, and floors.

TADELAKT
Tadelakt is a traditional Moroccan material
composed of lime plaster and olive-oil soap.
As the combined ingredients are waterproof,
tadelakt is ideal for bathrooms, shower
rooms, and kitchens; a tactile, seamless
alternative to tile, stone, or marble. The
structure of a tadelakt kitchen can be
constructed in brick and the surface applied
with layers of the plaster composite.

ADOBE
This ancient material dates back to the 8th
century BC. An adobe brick is a compacted
sun-dried mix of earth, straw, clay, and
moisture but it can also be poured or
'puddled' in layers to make a structure. In
arid climates, adobe buildings are impressively
resilient, for example the Pueblo architecture
of Taos or Santa Fe, New Mexico.

Interior designer and gallerist Denise Portmans sources work from sculptors, ceramicists, and painters whose pieces have an elemental feel that echoes her California home's desert setting. These tactile vessels and sculptures are by the French artist Pascale Vaquette.

A collage of encaustic tiles from Agnès Emery's Moroccan riad brings together a multitude of patterns united by a color palette of blue and white (opposite). Agnès's kitchen consists of a long counter with open shelving above it. The *batterie de cuisine* hung from a rail and piled onto the shelf is both decorative and practical (this page).

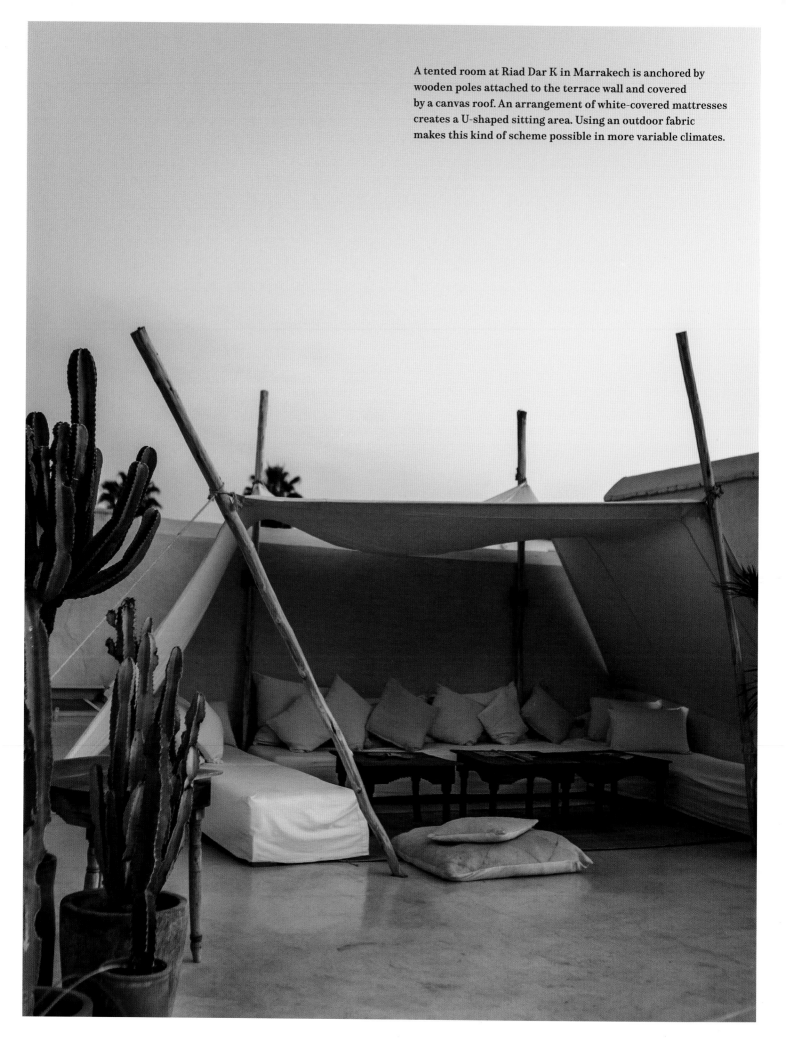

A tented room at Riad Dar K in Marrakech is anchored by wooden poles attached to the terrace wall and covered by a canvas roof. An arrangement of white-covered mattresses creates a U-shaped sitting area. Using an outdoor fabric makes this kind of scheme possible in more variable climates.

ROOMS WITH A VIEW

Blurring the boundaries between indoor living and life lived in the great outdoors is often part of the attraction of moving somewhere new, warmer, ideally somewhere with a mesmerizing view. English designer and shopkeeper Denise Portmans lives in Los Angeles, where the weather is always reliably clement, but her nomad getaway is in the Morongo Valley a couple of hours away, where temperatures fluctuate between 38°F/3.3°C and 100°F/38°C. In the winter it can be cold at night, but she has set up her home to take full advantage of the desert setting with stylish areas for dining, bathing, and cooking outside, extending the liveable footprint of the two-bedroom bungalow. A round plunge pool, a shower, and a 'bathroom' on the deck invite visitors to absorb the landscape at different times of day (with no neighbors to overlook anyone soaking in the concrete tub under the stars).

Moroccan riads are designed to allow for as much outdoor living as possible, with internal courtyards styled as flexible living spaces like Valérie Barkowski's at Dar Kawa. Positioned on the perimeter of the open garden, there are other rooms where the visitor can observe the orange trees while reclining on a wall-to-wall daybed partially open to the elements. The rooftop is the place to watch the sun rise or set from different seating arrangements; a low-slung mattress on a plastered platform or a group of 1960s classic canvas butterfly chairs. Agnès Emery has installed a velvet banquette-lined dining space behind billowing sky-blue voile curtains on her expansive white upper terrace, the perfect antidote to the multicolored claustrophobia of the medina.

Even a balcony can give an apartment dweller a welcome escape from confinement. Just add plants, a café table, chairs, and some outdoor lighting. Outdoor furniture can be as rudimentary or luxurious as you like. 'Performance' fabrics, which repel water and inhibit mold, combined with outdoor foam make upholstered mattresses, chairs, and canopies that stand up to wet weather, but slow-living nomads prefer the sensory comforts of hand-woven textiles sourced locally and teamed with vintage canvas military cots used as loungers.

Bamboo is strong but lightweight, making it ideal for furniture that can be moved from inside to out and employed as the framework for an impromptu shade structure, fixed with cable ties covered in garden twine. Take inspiration from the Mexican palapa, an outdoor room without walls or windows and incorporating built-in seating rather than sofas and chairs (which might blow away in a storm).

A *bhou* is a term for the Moroccan lounges you will find in a riad open to the internal courtyard. Here is the *bhou* at Riad 42 seen through a tangle of jasmine.

An outdoor kitchen makes eating and entertaining alfresco an easier proposition. Denise Portmans has added one along an outdoor wall of her property. Here she can prep meals without having to leave her guests.

OPEN KITCHEN

If your idea of outdoor cooking equipment is limited to a portable barbecue and a pair of long tongs, think again. An alfresco countertop, sink, and butcher's block combined in a work station make food preparation and dining into a communal experience. No longer is the chef confined to the indoor kitchen with a furtive glass of cooking sherry while everyone consumes pitchers of margaritas outside. This simple arrangement can be assembled inexpensively from a brick-built structure clad in tile or some kind of render (tadelakt, plaster, or concrete skim coat all work).

Every place has its palette. Here's one of the dominant color themes of North Africa: terracotta, a shade that engenders a feeling of warmth and comfort, a connection to the earth. This hue plays nicely with blues, emerald greens, or chrome yellow.

LOCAL COLOR –
A SENSE OF PLACE

Every fantasy house that I buy (and there are many) is an opportunity to create a new atmosphere. I never find shipping furniture to a new home very successful. Everything that I have lived with before proves to be too site-specific. If I could sell my houses including all fixtures and fittings, I would (I might take art with me, but that's it).

One of my favorite pastimes is discovering talented craftspeople, either virtually (Etsy is brimming with talent, and Instagram, too) or at local markets or stores when I travel. Flea markets and craft markets (even touristy ones) yield some great finds. I even like shopping in really horrible shops (dime stores, supermarkets, outlet stores) just to see if I can find one gem hiding in plain sight. This is extremely satisfying to me.

I must also recommend the absolute joy of a Mexican hardware store full of brightly colored brooms, buckets, and birdcages, or any proper hardware store for that matter. A 'DIY' person could create a home interior entirely from the contents. In Maine, I head to the ships' chandlers to buy rope, lighting, and utility fabrics. In Ireland, I discovered a shop that only sold locally woven wool tweed that could be used for clothing or upholstery (shades of *The Sound of Music* curtains turned into dirndl skirts). Imagine an ancient stone castle decorated with subtle tweeds and plaids. Rooting out the ingredients and tradespeople for your home will help you connect with the community and give any room you put together a sense of place.

If you are curious about shopping the Marrakech medina, employ a guide to help you navigate the best emporiums and help negotiate prices. There are also some excellent group shopping tours of Morocco (try @majesticdisorder), India, or Mexico, which arrange for visits to makers, souks, and markets and assistance with shipping purchases back home. Australian stylist Meg Morton leads style insider trips for a handful of interiors aficionados to all sorts of design meccas, from Paris to Tokyo and lots of places in between (check @theschoolinstagram for her updates about destinations).

When is a basket not a basket? When it's a sculpture. The floor in a SoHo loft is laid with a patchwork of *frazadas*, thick blankets from Peru (opposite). Denise Portmans mixes recycled cotton, heavy hand-woven linen, and raw silk in a bedroom at her Morongo Valley retreat in California (this page).

Color is a very personal matter. People tend to gravitate to either modulated neutrals or proper colors, but certain geographic locations will always be associated with particular shades. Pigments sourced locally, from the earth, from rocks, from flowers and plants, become those identifying colors. The American Southwest shares browns and terracottas with North Africa. Sky blue and white in combination is the palette of Tunisia and also of Greece. Scandinavian countries seem to prefer five thousand shades of gray and white to any saturated hues, probably because of the way northern light reacts to bright colors. Finding your palette is an intuitive process. Observe the available light in your interior and how it changes during the day. Consider the function and mood of each space you create and the flow of each shade from room to room.

An interpretation of Valentine Schlegel's interior style made for fashion label Malene Birger's new showroom. An installation by the designer Annaleena combines crisp white arches with sculptural ceramics (opposite). The wabi-sabi gypsum-covered wall with its handmade openings invites us to display objects and ceramics with similar primitive values (this page).

In Marrakech, rugs hanging from every rooftop, window, and wall create a gallery moved outdoors, layering pattern, color, and geometry on every structure.

Agnès Emery chose cooling shades of blue and green as an antidote to the heat of the medina (this page). Artichokes suggest a color scheme of purple and moss green; teal combines with plaster pink at Riad Baoussala; a wall painted in pinkish red limewash; turquoise zellige tiles line Agnès's kitchen walls (opposite clockwise from top left).

All my projects start with a mood board. It's easier to manifest a plan when you have assembled a mass of images, colors, and textures that conjure the feeling you are searching for, be it in a space or on a trip to somewhere new. You are an archive of everything you have seen and experienced, but externalizing the daydreams in your head will help ideas coalesce and develop.

HOW TO NOMAD

Butcher, baker, candlestick maker.....

At school 'careers' talks in my day, the only occupations suggested for linguists were interpreter or bilingual secretary; neither job appealed to me. As living abroad was my goal, I always made it my business to find out how people I met managed to make a living in a new country. Acquiring portable skills seemed key to migration. A fashion editor who married a diplomat was compelled to reconsider her career, as her new husband's job meant being posted from country to country every few years. Her clever and pragmatic move was to take up hairdressing, a job that introduced her to lots of people and quickly enhanced her social life wherever she landed. On a trip to Lisbon, I met a wine importer who establishes new networks by throwing pop-up dinner parties with local chefs. By connecting with talent and creating events, she combines work and play, expanding her circle of friends and clients.

Today we have the opportunity to do many jobs remotely. However, getting embedded in a culture is easier when you do something that takes you out and about, forcing you to speak the language and build a community. I have several friends who move between two or more countries, dealing in antiques/rugs/textiles or manufacturing furniture or clothing, a way of living that affords them flexibility and gives them their travel fix.

Hand-woven fishing nets from Gallipoli in Puglia transcend their practical purpose as sculptural objects (opposite). A bench at Masseria Potenti is softened with outdoor pillows in water-resistant Sunbrella fabrics (this page). Above a stone-topped console, beads from Tunisia hang from a hand-forged nail. The vase is Moroccan and the leaf is a dried 'elephant ear' from the NYC flower market (pages 52–53). An arched doorway in the Riad Dar K (page 54).

Perhaps the path isn't immediately obvious, but you might start out doing something that just allows you to move to a new country while working toward a grander plan. If you dream of living in a French château, it is possible to rehearse the experience when working as a guardian for an absent owner. Renting before buying is a good way to explore without commitment.

If your plan is to buy and renovate a property, it might make sense to turn this into income by renting out part of your house to travelers, creating a separate Airbnb or small hotel. Invest your time in creating a transportive space that allows fellow wanderers a slice of your fantasy.

THE WANDERERS

ANYWHERE BUT HERE

It has become apparent to me that you can divide people into two categories: Leavers or Remainers, Nomads or Stay-at-Homes. From a very early age, I knew that I was a Leaver. Every kind of journey was an opportunity for daydreaming, a blissful flow state as essential to the five-year-old me as it is to my current mental health. Sleepovers, school trips, even ghastly French exchanges had me turn on my heel with nary a backward glance at my parents. I was always ready for a new horizon and the invention of a new me. It is not, therefore, surprising that I have spent much of my life wondering where I should live, so much so that it rarely occurs to me to stay still.

High ceilings and sturdy chestnut beams make it simple to hang an egg-shaped rattan chair, softened with sheepskin pillows. Using floating furniture makes the space seem bigger and less crowded. The sunny bay window is the ideal spot to languish on a Scandinavian daybed that fits the space perfectly. Abstract shapes and layered natural textures are repeated throughout the room in art, textiles, and sculptural objects (opposite and this page).

I wanted to live in Amsterdam. It seemed a very reasonable place; bicycles, children efficiently transported atop bicycles, canals clean enough to swim in, recreational boating, cheese with jam for breakfast, flatness, nudity, tall men, tall women, art museums, big skies, seasons, flower fields, open sandwiches, pragmatism – all things that I like and value, having grown to love flatness at university in Norfolk, eastern England along with Siberian winds and chilly, empty beaches. Amsterdam seemed similar. And then there were my Scandinavian years, spent in Denmark, where I very much enjoyed a cheese-and-jam-for-breakfast lifestyle, a lack of topological undulation, lots of bicycles, *smørrebrød*, and so on.

Instead I manifested NYC, the New Amsterdam rather than the old, my manifestation compass being somewhat off that day, and became an accidental Slave of New York (though one of my favorite books, I wasn't aiming to reenact it). Coincidentally, I ended up living in the same apartment building as its author,

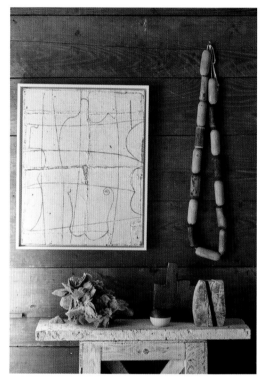

The Dutch door is the original entrance to the schoolhouse. The still life on the antique butcher's block includes a vase from Tunisia, a plaster plaque, and a handmade ceramic jug from a flea market filled with found feathers (left). A console combines a coral shelf and a painted plywood base. A painting by Rick Lewis echoes the sculptural shapes and tactile materials in every corner of the room. The wall wears a necklace of nautical wooden floats (below). A baker's rack is stacked with interiors magazines and found objects. The chain is part of a collaboration with Bloomist (opposite).

the high priestess of NYC Slaves, Tama Janowitz. Sadly, we did not become best friends or start a book club together, but I once helped her pick up all her groceries, which had tumbled out of their bags on the subway steps, and I believe she said 'Thanks' as she sped toward our shared lobby. Which really sums up my first few years in NYC: so near and yet so far.

In preparation for my new life in NYC, I had read to my three-year-old son Maira Kalman's deliciously illustrated Max books, depicting Max the tousled mutt living his best life with New York's Haute Bohemia at all the chicest salons, chewing pistachio-and-rose-petal macarons with hat designers and shoe critics, ballerinas and bullfighters. In my imagination, this escape to

Gotham would lead to a more glamorous, accomplished iteration of myself. I pictured myself attending Sex in the City-style soirées and the Met Ball, spending weekends in white clapboard houses on East Coast beaches, snapping my fingers at editorial meetings in a plate-glass tower, clicking down a wide marble corridor in wildly uncomfortable heels, perching some outré black spectacles on my nose. Alas, it wasn't like that at all (at first) and I soon learned that it is unwise to rely upon children's literature as a primer for an unknown city. Also, it should be noted that Woody Allen movies are practically documentaries.

We had a few years where we stumbled around trying to find our groove in our new 'home', sobbing into our Sancerre on Friday nights as we talked about Blighty.

The schoolhouse has chestnut walls and floors, which we sanded to lighten them. The pale indigo sofa provides the only 'color' in the room (pages 60–61). In the bedroom below the rafters, nomad elements include a papier-mâché elephant, a desk made from an old door, a bamboo lantern, and a chair by León León (these pages).

The 'Japandi' bathroom, with its concrete bathtub and cement board-panelled walls, was a labor of love. It took us a while to decide how to tackle it, but as we are 'soakers' we prioritized a tub with a view (this page). I prefer kitchens that don't scream 'kitchen', so this Canadian unfitted oak kitchen was the ideal solution. It is composed of separate pieces of freestanding furniture. We added the oak screen to create a pantry that hides a multitude of sins/stuff (opposite).

But slowly, gradually, we adapted. I was brave enough to order a sandwich with more than three ingredients and became less likely to spend as much time traveling backward as forward on the subway; we even bought a big American car and were able to afford that pinnacle of all luxuries, a weekend house in the Connecticut countryside (and a future needing double everything).

As you can imagine, finding the right house is no easy task when you are a couple of interiors buffs. It was my husband's 'turn' to decide upon this asset, so I prepared myself for a long and arduous search. Indeed, we cast about upstate and could not find anything. We attempted to buy enormous derelict houses that were not for sale, and some which were. And we found one that was perfect – too perfect. My husband, who relaxes by being extremely active, mending or building things, said he would have 'nothing to do' there. As I'm more of a horizontalist at weekends, I was looking for the opposite, a self-cleaning type of house, if possible.

However, one day we spied an intriguing undone sort of place with just enough eccentric, impractical corners, 'features', and 'potential'. And almost 4 acres/1.6 hectares to mow every weekend – how perfectly imperfect! It was an 1800 schoolhouse with a large kitchen extension/addition, an orangery, a crinkle-crankle wall (yes, really), and a tiny unfinished guest house. Yes please! Sign us up.

We didn't really have to debate this choice and bought it with no further ado. Digging around in the three-car garage (happy husband) we discovered that the house's original owners were a couple of photographers who worked in mid-century NYC for all the best magazines – Kismet! They had even left behind a vast archive of prints and negatives along with diaries and letters from such luminaries as Diana Vreeland. This was most definitely OUR place.

There were many things to do. It was probably the height of country chic to have unfinished orange pine walls in the 1960s, but I could not live with those.

The orangery's original doors had been replaced with ugly modern ones, so we added vintage French doors that we found at a flea market. In summer we move the bigger citrus trees outside (page 66). Martinis are served on a rusty table that came with the house. The clematis growing on the pool fence makes this spot especially dreamy (page 67). I have a bathing obsession and this is an 18th-century zinc Napoleonic campaign bathtub, found in Chicago (left). The orangery is used either as a dining room, or as an extra bedroom or workshop. We change it around all the time but the plants are always happy here (above and opposite).

The lofty kitchen extension was painted with many coats of white. My husband was content to spend weekends in a hazmat suit wielding the paint gun that I had lovingly purchased for him, while I reclined upon a sofa creating Pinterest boards for the more decorative aspects of the project. We left the chestnut-clad walls of the schoolhouse alone, but sanded its floors to a paler matte finish. We also left the slate flagstone floors in the kitchen, corridor, and bathroom untouched. The existing, rather basic kitchen cabinets were replaced with freestanding white oak ones by Coquo and marble tops made by the husband. We designed an 8-foot/2.5m kitchen table for the friends we would invite, and enlisted our friend Casey to make it.

The look we were aiming for could be summed up as European Modern Country, a blend of all the places where I had either lived or dreamed of living. Central to this look was the multipurpose space where everyone may witness the chaos of cooking dinner and the subsequent dereliction of the kitchen. The schoolhouse itself, connected to it by a glazed corridor, turned out to have the most magical light aspect. It is somehow always the right time to sprawl upon a sofa or daybed or hang in the rattan chair suspended from a beam and cocooned by sheepskins in this cozy room. There are two small bedrooms: one tucked away behind the fireplace on the ground floor and another in the roof beams above the living space.

The two-room guest house allows us a different atmosphere; a white-on-white space where I work at a painter's table and stare at the trees. Paintings in monochrome are by Alistair McCowan or found at flea markets and junk shops. The chubby chair is by Jack Rabbit Studio, a talented young designer discovered in Hudson, NY (opposite). The bathroom has its own wood-burning stove (right). I like to dress the bed in layers of wool and linen in shades inspired by the garden: rust, charcoal, cinnamon (far right).

THE LOOK WE WERE AIMING FOR COULD BE SUMMED UP AS EUROPEAN MODERN COUNTRY, A BLEND OF ALL THE PLACES WHERE I HAD EITHER LIVED OR DREAMED OF LIVING

Lucky guests are sequestered in the guest house, a glorified shed with its own freestanding bathtub.

While all this interior work was going on, we spent a large chunk of our budget on putting in a swimming pool. A pool! The very tippy-top of my childhood aspiration list was this indulgence. We designed one that was extremely simple, eschewing all the salesman's more ostentatious suggestions. After a terrifying estimate from a landscaper, my husband undertook the job himself with the help of the friendly local owner of a digger. Planting was to be in the style of Piet Oudolf (or how we interpreted the master on our modest budget) with much advice from our garden muse, Lindsey Taylor.

The majority of this makeover took place within the first few years, but we dragged our feet when it came to the orangery and main bathroom. The red gloss-painted bathroom, as sturdily built as a tank, took much willpower to demolish and even Mr. Fixit had a defeated look about him when he disappeared for yet another dusty weekend with his sledgehammer. The result is a triumph of his

ingenuity; somewhat Japanese in atmosphere, it has a concrete egg-shaped tub, walls clad in cement board, and an elongated trough sink made in Petit Granit.

Our very last project was the orangery, where we committed NY sacrilege and painted over the brick walls with homemade white limewash. We did keep the wonderful brick floor, though, which was relaid perfectly by another friend, Jesse. Home to a jungle of orphaned plants left over from photo shoots, this space is now accessed by a secret door, another of Mr. Fixit's excellent ideas.

If you were to drop in one weekend, you might happen upon our Bohemian salon in action, in the style of the Bloomsbury Group but without the complicated triangular relationships. Shoe critics, tango dancers, celebrated minimalism coaches all gather here to document alfresco picnics involving violet macarons and wild-crafted kombucha. We compare notes about our travels, where we've been and where we are going to next; Tuscany or Tripoli, Porto or Patagonia, wherever we can create that elusive rest home for retired nomads.

AGNÈS IN WONDERLAND

Architect Agnès Emery sends a colleague to collect us from an agreed point five minutes from her home; so convoluted is the tangle of alleys that take you there that even our local guide is confounded. Agnès claims to know the way with her eyes shut (although once, arriving very late, she attempted to enter the home of a previously unknown neighbor who promptly directed her to the correct door).

Grand dame of tile, textile, highly pigmented paint, and sinuous iron furniture, Agnès Emery has been working in Marrakech for 30 years. Her relationship with Morocco is pivotal to her business and so she arrives here once a month to direct or collaborate with the artisans who make her products. 'You don't end up with what you wanted but something else, and that is good too,' she says sagely. Her base here, two connected houses with a layout as complex as an Escher drawing, serves as showroom, canvas, and laboratory for her ideas. The entire space, bar one eggplant bedroom, is decorated in every shade of blue and green imaginable; a highly effective rebuttal of the saying 'blue and green should never be seen'. She chose the palette as a refreshing contrast to the heat and dust of the medina, and the effect has the feel of a fairytale; an oasis fortress built for a landlocked mermaid.

Agnès's cavernous masterpiece, with its multiple stairways, courtyards, and galleries, is entirely devoted to her experiments with both the intense solid colors, sublime in their variation of shade, and her cement patterned tile. The *carrelages* cover the floors and creep up

The original meaning of 'riad' is an internal courtyard garden, a feature common to Moorish architecture. Houses are constructed with rooms that look onto a cooling garden oasis (right). **On the mezzanine, a long book-lined study opens onto the balcony above the courtyard** (opposite).

A bathroom is tiled in Agnès's zellige tiles glazed in a shade that varies from eau de Nil to pale lilac. Handmade and imperfect, each tile is unique (above). Encaustic tiles form a decorative panel in the center of this floor. Colored cements are poured into the different sections of a metal mold to make the patterns (opposite).

the walls, changes of pattern deftly orchestrated between outdoor and indoor spaces. A shallow pond is tiled in a fish pattern, and mirror tiles imitating fish scales surround a mirror and catch the light in one of the velvet-upholstered dens, while green alphabet tiles cover another den floor. The total commitment to color, a deep dive into a peacock-hued universe, has a singular and magical effect, seducing any visitor into viscerally understanding the sensory fulfillment that decoration in bold, saturated color can bring.

Agnès makes a range of highly pigmented casein paints that are breathable, washable, and matte in texture. This bedroom combines an Asian armoire (opposite), a graphic striped bedcover, and a sinuous metal bedhead attached to the wall, her own design (this page).

The salon plays with texture and shades of green and turquoise to magical effect, mixing glass tiles that mimic the iridescence of fish scales with encaustic pattern and devoré velvet cushions. Low banquettes make ideal, space-saving seating in narrow rooms looking onto the courtyard (left and opposite). The elongated kitchen is built from a run of tiled counter integrated with painted cupboard doors. Modulated turquoise zellige tiles stretch up to the ceiling (pages 80-81).

Finding the original house was a lengthy process; Agnès saw about a hundred houses with three different agents before the fourth brought her here. A few years later she bought the second house, which is now connected by a slim passageway. The temperature and season dictates where Agnès spends her time; rather than being dedicated to a single purpose these spaces are intended to be flexible. Summer days are mostly spent on the ground floor, but in winter she escapes to the rooftop for some sunshine and a view of the Red City's patchwork of terraces.

On the day of our February shoot, Agnès is ensconced in her book-lined study, which stretches along an upstairs gallery open to the courtyard. She has just arrived from Brussels and is opening the house from its winter sleep. Her team assembles lunch in the long galley kitchen tiled in turquoise and piled high with tin trays, teapots, tea glasses, and ceramics. We eat around a table in the courtyard and then roam around the labyrinth capturing as much aquatic beauty as we can, searching for a glimpse of that elusive mermaid.

The whitewashed rooftop includes a room
open to the elements where printed voile
curtain panels flutter in the breeze (opposite).
Marrakech's medina has no trees, but Agnès
incorporated some stylized ones into the
wrought-iron gate (this page).

NO PLACE LIKE ROME

After consulting numerous nomads, I have discovered that a certain mindset is required for a successful transition; dithering or clinging, however limply, to home will only end in a half-lived adventure. Nothing but full immersion will do. If you don't speak the language, learn it fast. Open up! Join in! Make a fool of yourself! Otherwise, you risk hovering on the edges of the new place or creating your own expatriate island.

Liselotte Watkins' nomad story is one that I have heard many times. It's the 'leaving early' story of a youthful iconoclast, a 'throws-caution-to-the-wind' type of gypsy, who picks up their bags and follows something or someone without a backward glance, too young to question the sagacity of such a move. Imagine leaving Sweden for Texas at 17, with 'no money, no plan'. 'The worst-case scenario was going back,' says Liselotte. 'I was a sponge ready to soak it all up.' A full-immersion nomad indeed.

Quitting Texas, she headed to NYC while her then boyfriend went back to Sweden, promising to return. She landed at the YWCA on 14th Street opposite the Chelsea Hotel, a hip-adjacent address ideal for a neophyte New Yorker. Chance meetings, surviving from day to day, from gig to gig, meant operating in the present tense. 'Days went by and you were a winner for still being there.'

After making friends with an art director who worked for Barneys, the temple of NY chic, Liselotte turned her hand to illustrating the store's weekly beauty

The dining room, between the kitchen and living room, is open to both rooms; an ideal layout for family life. Hung salon-style with paintings, this room shares the 'every-shade-goes' color scheme of the apartment; citrus shades combined with greens and blues (opposite). Liselotte uses the traditional shapes of found vessels as canvases for her Cubist paintings (right).

Paintings found at flea markets line the walls of the diminutive dining room (left). In the entrance hall, a console table is used to display books and objects (below). A collection of signature orange Hermès boxes appears repeatedly on tables and shelves throughout. No flower can compete with the bright patterns of Liselotte's vases; simple grasses are the perfect foil for the extravagance of the dancing patterns (opposite).

HER DISTINCTIVE PALETTE FIZZES THROUGH
ALL HER WORK AND CELEBRATES THE OBSESSIONS
AND RITUALS OF HER CHOSEN COUNTRY

ads for *The New York Times*. The boyfriend did not return, but fashion illustration stuck. Liselotte met another Swede, now her husband, who whisked her to Paris where she had her first child and then another in quick succession. But before she could settle into a Parisian life, they moved to Milan and her Italian odyssey began.

In terms of color temperature, I think of Sweden as monochrome and Italy as a rainbow. Considering Liselotte's Rome apartment, which throbs with citrus yellow and tangerine, it's clear that she feels exuberantly at home in her Roman setting.

The kitchen, dining room, and sitting room are separate spaces but they are all connected on one side of the apartment. The galley kitchen is brightly accessorized with Liselotte's illustrated plates combined with monochromatic Fornasetti and other vintage ceramics on the wall (this page and opposite).

She has a wardrobe full of La DoubleJ maximalist patterned silk dresses in shades of everything. Her distinctive palette fizzes through all her work, from the bold vessels on which she paints stylized female characters and Cubist patterns, to the recent larger-scale paintings in soft sherbet shades painted during the pandemic for a solo show at the Swedish Millesgården gallery. These depict detailed interiors inhabited by voluptuous female figures: mothers, goddesses, and their offspring, imaginary characters drawn from her observations of Italy and the Italian way of life. Liselotte, the outsider, celebrates the obsessions and rituals of her chosen country; the Italian predilection for routine, tradition, craft, food, and, of course, style.

Unsurprisingly, the tender domestic scenes are in sync with her 19th-century apartment, where a centrally located dining room connects on one side with a wedge-shaped sitting room singing with sunshine yellow and on the other to a simple white kitchen where

Chrome yellow is the predominant 'happy' color in Liselotte's decorating palette. She appreciates the color for its sunny vibe, which provokes fond memories of her grandmother's summerhouse in Sweden (this page and opposite).

Liselotte's colorful ceramics add a decorative flourish. 'Homemaking or nesting is my coping mechanism,' she explains. It's a feeling that she wants to create rather than a particular style, aiming for a sunny vibe that reminds her of her grandmother's Swedish summerhouse. Even in this discreetly bourgeois neighborhood (the apartment looks onto the grand façades of embassies), Watkins will shout '*Buongiorno!*' to locals as protocol demands. 'Community is important here,' she says. 'You have to make the effort.'

Her roots may have grown in Rome, but recent events have allowed the family to spend time in the Tuscan countryside near Siena, where they are renovating a house. Like many others temporarily set free from metropolitan life due to the pandemic, they have thrived in a bucolic setting; Liselotte's daughter is able to ride horses there and she paints in her spacious studio, easing the transition of her work from commercial fashion illustration to fine art. In fact, the family has adapted so easily to country life that they plan to give up city living for this version of *la dolce vita*, another colorful full immersion.

A collage of influences and ideas: illustrations, works in progress, and signature plates gathered on the hexagonal tiles of Liselotte's living-room floor (pages 92–93). **The entrance hall boasts an irreverent mix of mid-century sideboard, 19th-century chandelier, and taxidermy antelope** (opposite). **Hundis the dachshund relaxes on a mid-century chair** (above).

A patchwork quilt in the master bedroom extends the theme of Liselotte's graphic paintings, which flank the masculine iron bedstead. She eschews bedside storage in favor of chairs stacked high with bedtime reading matter.

LESS IS MOORE

Minimalists tend to evolve in one direction.
They pare down, they need less and want less,
and, if they are really good, they convince
even the most covetous maximalist that they
have got it all wrong.

Interior designer September Moore might be described as
a minimalist, an essentialist, perhaps as an exponent of
'slow design'; whatever the term, she's a dab hand at
creating an elegant atmosphere with simple ingredients,
and has a way with materials that makes the idea of extra
layers rather superfluous. Her rooms, always in ancient
French buildings, are the decorating equivalent of *le mot
juste*, poetic in their simplicity and somehow just 'right'.

   Ironically, when I visited her at her last home,
Camellas Lloret, a *chambre d'hôte* in the Languedoc that
she ran with her husband and design collaborator Colin
Moore, it became part of my book about collections and
collectors, *The Stuff of Life*. Three years ago, the Moores
sold that business from their evocative Instagram images
(including much of their 'stuff') and moved into a house
on the same street that they had previously used for
Colin's chiropractic practice. They then acquired a second
house on the corner of that same street, Rue de l'Angle
(now available for rentals), just a few yards away, and have
been renovating both properties simultaneously.

**The monochromatic living room couldn't be more pared down.
Chalky limewashed walls (Balance by Bauwerk Colour), linen
slipcovers, and a pale terracotta tiled floor are all that's needed
for an effortlessly stylish but comfortable room** (opposite).
**Layers of paint scraped from the woodwork revealed pale
green shades that bring the outdoors in** (this page). **An
internal lightwell is a novel place to keep a group of cacti in
terracotta pots, adding more shades of green** (right).

Rough luxe good looks are achieved with earthy materials; unvarnished wood, raw concrete, and limewash are unpretentious and timeless. The front door opens directly into a kitchen and dining room (pages 100 and 101).

None of this explains their nomadic credentials – the recent 'micro-move' across the street an anomaly in a series of bigger migrations – but the Moores have always made bold decisions about where to live and work. They met, rather romantically, on a train a couple of decades ago when September, having finished art school and fled the US, where she had always felt out of place, was on her way to create a new European life in Paris and Italy with her best friend, a model.

Instead of Milan, where she was supposed to start work as a fashion stylist, she ended up in South Africa with Colin, loved it, and stayed for four years. Next they 'nomaded around' the States for some years: Jackson, Atlanta, and Tampa, Florida where they settled in the absurdly named New Suburb Beautiful. While Colin was developing his career as a chiropractor, September was working with renowned garden designer Ryan Gainey, which led to setting up her own store, Into the Garden, which sold everything for outdoor garden spaces and garden-inflected interiors.

The serene living room is a level beneath the dining room and looks out onto the street below (this page). September made a tiled mobile planter for her rubber tree and chose an oversized linen sofa that takes up the whole width of the room (opposite).

SEPTEMBER'S TRADEMARK COLORS HAVE ALWAYS BEEN
THOSE MUTED, CHALKY, SUBTLE SHADES REMINISCENT OF
CÉZANNE LANDSCAPES OR MORANDI STILL LIFES

Moving away from her usual palette of greenish hues, September worked with friend Bronwyn Riedel of Bauwerk Colour to find the right shades for this house. The largest bedroom is enveloped in Marrakech, a dusty peach shade that adds a pale sunset glow to the minimally furnished space. The rough-hewn bed is dressed in natural linen and flanked by tree-stump tables (these pages and pages 104–105).

This enterprise meant that they could develop and maintain their old-world aesthetic with buying trips to European flea markets. Always a reluctant Floridian, September was determined to make a permanent return to Europe and so the couple (now with three children in in tow) decided to settle in Montpellier, renting an apartment for a couple of years before their first big house renovations in Uzès and Baron, where they spent five years in each house before moving to their current base, sleepy Montréal, 20 minutes away from Carcassonne.

September's trademark colors have always been those muted, chalky, subtle shades reminiscent of Cézanne landscapes or Morandi still lifes. Working on the new house, received in a 'deplorable' state, was no exception. But this time she was tempted to veer away from her favorite greenish tones to embrace earthy hues; think pale Moroccan pinks and adobe browns. 'Color became the starting point for this house,' she explains. Her friend Bronwyn Riedel, 'color genius' and joint founder of Bauwerk Colour, happened to be visiting and was able to ease September into the new palette, directing her

September's office is a tranquil space with a view of the treetops, that flash of green that brings rooms alive (this page). As a texture break from limewash, the Moores added a wall of thin wooden planks (opposite). The paper globe, the minimalist's go-to lampshade, appears in every shape and size.

A kitchen built in plywood rounds out the essentialist look. September insists that a smaller kitchen is easy to work in, with everything close to hand. (opposite). The upstairs shower room combines concrete, wood, and terracotta with a black-framed mirror and wall lights (above). The triangular balcony has just enough space for a café table (right).

toward Bauwerk's textural limewash paints, using four different shades from concrete grey to the palest flesh tint (Balance in the dining room, the kitchen is Chickpea, and Smokebush in the living room and bathroom).

The rest of the redesign is also about materials; a raw plywood kitchen, a concrete and plaster shower room with its original doors stripped and scraped revealing just traces of older paint layers, floors tiled with tactile terracotta octagons or retaining original patterned tile. The furniture selection could not be more edited and pared down; a monolithic linen sofa that works as an office, bed, and gathering space in the living room, the two bedrooms monastic with their primitive wooden bed frames and wool futon mattresses, the kitchen tiny but easy to work in. However, as a whole the feeling imparted here is that of intense wellbeing. One wonders what else could a room possibly need when it is this comfortable?

Along the way the Moores have become enviably self-sufficient; between them they can tackle many hardcore renovation tasks themselves. When it comes to furniture and lighting, September's current mantra is 'find it (vintage), build it, or make it'. She has set up her other kitchen as a kind of atelier where she works dyeing antique linen and sewing on her machine, which sits at the kitchen table opposite shelves stacked with the ingredients and tools necessary for her projects.

Although they have now been settled on this one street in France for more than a decade, the Moores are constantly on the hunt for other ruins worthy of their touch. Nomads to the core, now that their children have all grown up and migrated elsewhere, the couple are planning to spend time in another country they love, Spain, where another beautiful wreck currently awaits its rough luxe makeover.

NOMADSLAND

Dominique sighs a Gallic sigh when she hears our travel plans. We left Marrakech at sunrise, just as the market vendors were beginning to stir, steam rising from the tea carts, a background soundtrack of muezzin and the whine of mopeds zipping around the lanes. Our guide led us through shadowy passages to the gates of the medina to find our taxi to Essaouira, the Atlantic beach destination three hours from Marrakech beloved by both surfers and travelers. Our journey is more of an extended day trip, which we are already beginning to regret. Dominique created this place for siestas, not schedules.

Set slightly apart from the guest complex, Dominique's own home makes the most of the peaceful, bucolic setting with an outdoor dining set-up by the pool shaded by a bamboo roof and built-in banquette seating on the opposite side (opposite). **The terracotta tadelakt chimneypiece in the living/sitting/dining area for guests incorporates cubbyholes for books** (above right).

At her riad, Baoussala, you may breakfast at any time of day. And there are plenty of comfortably appointed corners to escape to for a nap, a turquoise swimming pool glitters invitingly, or you might stretch out on one of the many banquette sofas strewn with pillows that are dotted about the place. There will be home-cooked food prepared by her chef, a clay wood-burning stove to gather around should the winds turn chilly, a library of novels in many languages haphazardly stacked in a wabi-sabi tadelakt bookshelf curving around the stove in the room that serves as a combined dining/kitchen living area.

If color is your thing, the sprawling compound will be your nirvana: a terracotta cave, a rose-pink tower, an Yves Klein-blue amphitheater; rooms painted in saturated shades of emerald green or sugared-almond pink, textiles in violet, terracotta, ruby red, and citrus hues. The decoration is unpretentious yet considered; curtains are

The ground floor comprises an L-shaped combined kitchen and sitting room. Concrete stairs lead up to a large bedroom and study with far-reaching views (above). **The tactile kitchen mixes copper backsplash, wooden drawers, and cast-concrete countertops** (opposite).

made from local textiles thrown over bamboo poles, and tiled floors are warmed with the ubiquitous Moroccan rugs.

The eucalyptus trees rustle in the sea breeze leaving heaps of leaves on the ground, gathering into drifts in every crevice. The view from this flat landscape, which stretches for miles, is agricultural: farmsteads and donkeys, a windmill or two. Baoussala is 5½ miles/9km from the beach 'but not lost', says our host. Dominique and her husband Bruno worked with local builders and craftsmen to create a series of buildings inspired equally by Berber, African, and Mexican architecture. 'This is not *une maison sérieuse*,' she insists. 'It is a fantasy.' Her intention was to create somewhere welcoming where guests might easily slide into a gentler rhythm, where they might be contentedly alone or socialize with other guests. Within this intriguing compound you might find yourself walking in circles, since the organically evolving layout is as capricious as it is creative.

The integrated seating area combines two levels: one for sitting and the upper level for reclining upon. Dominique added traditional Moroccan painted tea tables and Mexican chairs (these pages). There are many opportunities for sprawling on an outdoor sofa at Baossala. Here a blue bench is loaded with faded red and violet cushions (page 118). The arched cave is another semi-outdoor retreat (page 119).

HER INTENTION WAS TO CREATE SOMEWHERE WELCOMING WHERE GUESTS
MIGHT EASILY SLIDE INTO A GENTLER RHYTHM, WHERE THEY MIGHT BE
CONTENTEDLY ALONE OR SOCIALIZE WITH OTHER GUESTS

About 22 years ago, Dominique came here as an escape from a life spent in Paris and Burgundy and in search of a concept the French call *bien-être*. Her plan was to live by the sea in a way that would connect both home and work. She wanted to build from scratch and was looking for the right place. Essaouira seduced her. 'Sometimes you need to stop thinking,' she advises sagely. The Baoussala team that she built became a second family; her assistant Léah has been with her for 12 years. She emphasizes the importance of adapting to the Moroccan culture rather than imposing upon it. It's the nomad's duty to do the adjusting, not the other way around.

Dominique has built her own house, separate from the communal quarters, with a terrace, outdoor living room, and an upstairs office that affords far-reaching views. Living here, she says, has helped her to appreciate pleasures as simple as breakfast eaten outside in the sunshine, walks to the beach with her dog Loco, and exercising with trainer Abdel, a routine she never misses. When she needs an injection of metropolitan life she flies direct to Paris from Essaouira, a contrast she appreciates, but nowadays she identifies as a 'Saouira'. She has grown roots here.

Dominique's mission is disarmingly uncomplicated: to soothe the world-weary and the sleep-deprived with the gentleness of this atmosphere, to share the whisper of the eucalyptus and the luminosity of the light, to convert hectic travelers into sybarites.

Painting the lower third of the walls a stronger color is a way to unite two separate but connected rooms. In a sitting room, a tadelakt-plastered fireplace provides warmth on cooler evenings. Dominique has combined a mid-century Eero Saarinen table with primitive stools and a colonial daybed. Other shades of green and teal and a violet throw turn a simple divan into a sofa. (pages 120-121 and opposite). Shades of Yves Klein blue and peacock green appear throughout the riad, a thread that unites indoor and outdoor spaces (above and page 125).

A roof deck is tiled in indigo and white encaustic tiles. The space is edged by a low terracotta ledge, somewhere to perch, drink tea, and watch the sunset (this page).

MEDINA IN MONOCHROME

The Marrakech medina might not be the most obvious home for a monochromist with modernist tendencies. Here, the briefest sortie into the spice market is a maximalist's dream-dive into sensory overload, the saturated piles of spices and pigments, the dizzying multihued geometry of rugs, djellabas, scarves, baskets, and kaftans screaming for attention at every turn. But while Boho-gypset devotees come here to luxuriate in the louche, layered decorative styling of the El Fenn or Secret Souk hotels, discerning travelers with more sober (but undeniably sophisticated) tastes might feel more at home in Valérie Barkowski's riad Dar Kawa, a calm 17th-century oasis of white accented with black, where the peace of the internal courtyard is disturbed only by the soft thud of oranges tumbling off trees, or the muezzin's haunting call to prayer at dawn, noon, mid-afternoon, sunset, and nightfall.

In the central courtyard at Dar Kawa, Valérie mixes mid-century Bertoia chairs softened with sheepskins with a simple white slipcovered sofa in a traditional shape (opposite). The monochromatic embroidered textiles are from her textile collections, which she sells from her V.barkowski store in the medina. A rooftop sitting area with far-reaching views of all the neighboring terraces is the perfect place for taking in the sunset (above right).

Valérie, a restless student bored by the confines of conventional education, started to travel after quitting art school to work as a model. The job suited her as it facilitated a peripatetic lifestyle where she could take time to dig into the cities that attracted her: Chiang Mai, New York, Ho Chi Minh City, and more. A wanderer at heart, Valérie found she was able to feel at home anywhere; 'As long as there are artisans, interesting cultural places, and good food, I am fine,' she qualifies. Her approach to a new place is to 'melt into' it, seeking to absorb the vibe and match the rhythm, taking her lead from the locals.

The tadelakt application rises several inches up the wall, functioning as a seamless alternative to a baseboard (this page). Usually meals are eaten in the courtyard, but for cooler days there's an indoor dining space hidden behind a white curtain. Walls are hung with framed black and white photographs (opposite).

It was during three years spent living in Russia that Valérie found her métier. When she needed household linens but could not find them apart from linen yardage, she employed 'babushkas' to sew and embroider for her. Admiring friends soon started to commission pieces from her, and this developed into Twist The World, which aptly describes her mission to discover and reimagine 'ancestral textiles' and local crafts with an approach that modernizes, edits, and simplifies, adding Valérie's own 'twist'.

In 1991, she found herself in Morocco, a country that 'had not been on my travel map' and fell under its spell, vowing to return to live when she could. Five years later, she started to look at riads in Marrakech, a process she found addictive.

The arched Moorish doors are all painted a flat battleship gray, a shade that echoes the color of the polished tadelakt floors (opposite). **An entire room is devoted to lounging, with a mattress covered with a traditional Moorish wedding blanket and piles of embroidered pillows** (this page).

No two were alike and many didn't have the
paperwork required for purchase. Dar Kawa
was a wreck but had a compelling atmosphere
and beautiful proportions, and exuded a
'feeling of *bien-être*'. Valérie set to work with
an architect friend to make a home with four
suites for guests, a shaded rooftop garden for
lounging, and that dreamy courtyard, which
serves as an outdoor living and dining room.

The riad is furnished with a typically
light touch and an eye for unexpected
juxtapositions; monochromatic bed and table
linens and graphic pillows from Valérie's
range mix with sequin-laden Moroccan
wedding blankets, mid-century white Bertoia
chairs, and bowler-hat lampshades. In the
bedrooms, stacks of vintage leather suitcases
and dark lacquered chests add contrasting
heft and texture. Surfaces are tactile, the
bathrooms making use of local tadelakt
(the versatile lime-based plaster finished with
olive-oil soap to render it waterproof), but
also mosaic and zellige tiles. Valérie explains
that the neutral palette allows her to make
changes to the interior styling very easily.
'Also, in Morocco you don't live the same
way in summer and winter. In summer,
you live on the terrace in the early morning
and evening as you hunt for some fresh air.
Winters are the reverse.'

**One of the riad's five bedrooms has its own
daybed seating area for drinking tea or reading.
Valérie updates boho-souk style by employing
graphic repetitions; for example, three identical
wooden tables and three pillows** (right).

Gray tadelakt walls are waterproofed with olive-oil soap, making the material ideal for a kitchen or bathroom (page 134). Hand-carved lemonwood spoons made locally are installed in a sculptural group (page 135). Primitive shapes in carved wood or clay are gathered on window sills or nestled together on the floor (opposite and this page).

At one point, Valérie's textile business became so successful that the balance of her life felt out of whack and far from what she had set out to do. Working with 500 embroiderers and knitters and more than 400 distributors scattered all over the world, she no longer knew all the people she employed, which felt alien to her. Realizing that she was not 'formatted' to feed fashion's demand for seasonal collections, she sold the brand and recalibrated to life lived at a slower pace with time for daydreaming or napping on the terrace and a flexible schedule.

To live as a nomad is to embrace the seasons, the possibility of change, of serendipitous meetings. With her workshop, Marrakech shop, riad, and online store, Valérie has managed to create both a home and a source of income, which anchors her and allows her to roam.

The riad's color scheme might be strictly edited, but Valérie is not afraid to mix pattern with bold embroidery, striped dhurries, and Berber rugs layered in this bedroom suite. The sofa looks onto the internal courtyard below.

Crisp white bed linens are embellished with Valérie's Twist The World touches: contrasting black hems, blanket-stitched edges, and running-stitch patterns (opposite). **Black tassels borrowed from Moroccan fez hats serve as pulls for light switches** (this page).

THE RIAD IS FURNISHED WITH
A TYPICALLY LIGHT TOUCH AND AN EYE
FOR UNEXPECTED JUXTAPOSITIONS

MARCEL PROUST   L'INDIFFÉRENT

folio   Pierre Assouline   Grâces lui soient rendues   3999

folio   Albert Cohen   Ô vous, frères humains   191

folio   Tchekhov   Le Duel et autres nouvelles   1433

folio   Duras   Les petits chevaux de Tarquinia   187

folio   Kafka   La métamorphose   74

folio   Jacques Prévert   Spectacle   104

BERNARD-MARIE KOLTÈS   COMBAT DE NÈGRE ET DE CHIENS   MINUIT

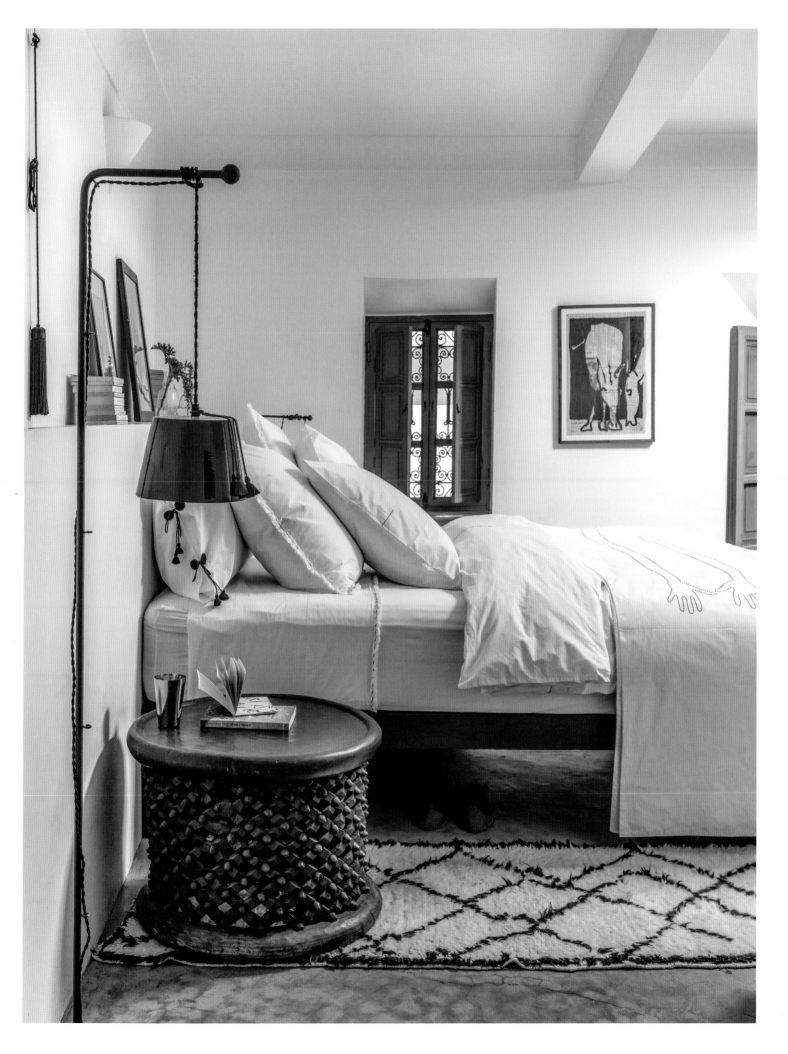

DESERT HEARTS

'I've found your house,' Denise Portmans' friend insisted, sending her a picture of a buttercup-yellow door. With characteristic decisiveness Denise, who had been searching for a desert escape for three years, put in an offer sight unseen and now Merchant House in California's Morongo Valley is part of an idiosyncratic design company including Denise and her daughter Sara's gallery/shop in Venice and a refitted Airstream with outdoor kitchen and plunge pool in Joshua Tree, CA.

'When I saw the house two weeks later, I walked in and cried,' Denise admits, simultaneously excited and daunted by the renovation of the three-bedroom, one-level house surrounded by 5 acres/2 hectares of rocky scrubland, Palo Santo trees, and an arid, undulating desert landscape that needed to be cleared of random accumulated garbage.

'The bones were already there,' says Portmans, who found local builders to add concrete floors outdoors and sliding glass doors that would connect inside with outside, orchestrating that all-important 'flow'. At the height of the desert heat (often well over 100°F/38°C), outdoor living is only comfortable in the evenings, which Denise and friends spend around a long dining table under a shady

Denise's desert location is filled with works by the artists that she showcases in her Los Angeles store. The canvas and plaster painting is by her daughter and collaborator Sara Marlowe Hall (opposite). **Rugs from the Atlas Mountains, mid-century chairs, and studio pottery are the building blocks of Merchant style** (above right).

gable. She has also taken to bathing alfresco, with an ovoid concrete tub on the upper deck, a circular plunge pool with mountain views, and an outdoor shower.

The arched yellow door with its distinctive decorative brass hinges and oversized latch remains, an enticing entrance that transports the visitor to Africa or perhaps Moorish-influenced Andalusia. The long porch beyond the door extends this impression, with its white-on-white sitting area, a combination of built-in banquettes covered with Moroccan wedding blankets and handwoven striped pillows that you might find in any global nomad's stylish interior, from Mallorca to Marrakech. Denise has layered sculptures, wabi-sabi ceramics, sculptural lighting, mobiles; all objects that conjure her signature look. 'It's a living, breathing house/gallery,' she explains. Should a guest take a shine to something here, they may purchase it or even commission the Merchant duo to tackle their entire home.

Even the opening into Denise's kitchen is sculptural;
a clever way to connect to the living room without
revealing too much (opposite). Lila Roo's sculptural
tapestry, made from repurposed plastic, hangs in the
dining area. Roo is one of the artists shown at Denise's
Merchant Gallery in LA (this page).

The look achieved is deliberately loose, an amalgamation of journeys to flea markets, thrift stores, artists' studios – totems of a life of exploration.

Denise grew up in London with a painter and ceramicist mother who ignited her taste for soulful handmade objects, sculpture, and paintings and a penchant for an earthy color palette of warm neutrals: ocher, khaki, indigo. She would spend weekends with her mother and sister wandering around Biba, Barbara Hulanicki's iconic Kensington boutique, or Casa Pupo, the 1970s decorating mecca known for its OTT white ceramic lamps, faux bamboo furniture, and giant potted palms. With a head full of these design references, Denise headed to New York and LA to work as a fashion stylist and eventually started the wildly successful Gotta Have It in Venice, the city's first vintage consignment store.

Denise layers her beds with a patchwork of textiles, from indigo to dyed recycled mustard cotton by Suay, an LA business that repairs, dyes, and makes pieces from discarded fabric that might otherwise end up in landfill (opposite). A closet has lost its doors, putting the contents on display. There's just enough space to slot in a mid-century dresser (this page).

In the living room, ceramics on a window sill are silhouetted against calico curtains, which shade the room from the desert heat (this page). A vintage limestone sculpture, Pascale Vaquette's ceramic sculpture, and a wall hanging by Claudia Pearson are grouped between arched windows in the sun porch entrance to the house (opposite).

Morocco in Morongo: in the porch room, banquette seats strewn with piles of pillows and covered with a Moroccan wedding blanket conjure a nomad atmosphere.

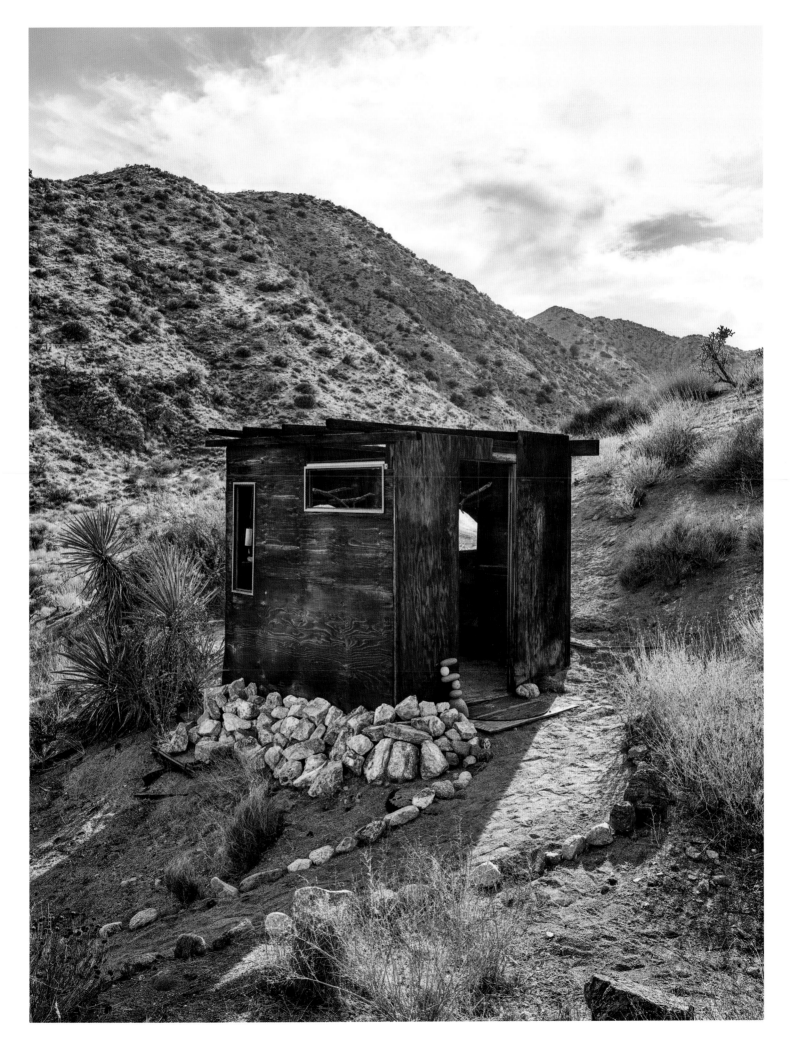

In order to make the most of
the desert setting, Denise made
several additions, including an
outdoor kitchen and dining area
(opposite and right). **Other outdoor
rooms are staged for soaking, with
a plunge pool, a shower, and even a
bathtub** (pages 152, 153, and 156–157).

Midlife is often a catalyst for change and in her fifties Denise felt ready for a new challenge. Seven years ago, she opened a pop-up interiors gallery-cum-store with her artist daughter Sara Marlowe Hall. In order to source stock, they took an investigative trip to the Atlas Mountains to buy rugs, an adventure arranged by a 'friend of a friend'. At some points they wondered if they would ever receive the rugs they had bought there, but the merchandise arrived as promised. The enterprise proved successful enough for the pop-up to morph into a permanent space on Lincoln Boulevard, Los Angeles.

Denise relishes the time that she is able to spend in the desert, but she is also based in Venice, CA where she lives in a 1908 Craftsman-style clapboard house, close to her store and the beach. In common with many 'transplants' she often pines for European culture and rainy days, considering Los Angeles a 'young person's city'. But for the moment she seems to have achieved a rare balance between work and play, two homes that complement each other, the grand isolation of the desert and the laid-back buzz of her city neighborhood both facilitating her Merchant lifestyle.

ROCK THE KASBAH

If Anita Pallenberg had run away to Sicily with a Moroccan rug
dealer and a clutch of Murano chandeliers, she might have set up
digs rather like Marie Olsson Nylander's latest (and perhaps greatest)
renovation project. Palazzo Cirillo in Sicily is a perfectly rhapsodic
mash-up of Biba-meets-souk chic befitting a professional nomad.

The serial renovator's romantic acquisition occupies a
rather unlikely position for a 'palazzo', its noble, dusty-rose
plaster facade wedged incongruously between two mid-
century apartment buildings on a narrow street that may
only be reached by cars as neatly proportioned as a Fiat
Cinquecento. The 'Sleeping Beauty', situated in a working-
class seaside town (once a manufacturing base for Fiat
cars), had been empty for 30 years before Marie discovered
it on a speculative house-hunting trip to Sicily with her
skeptical husband in 2017.

With five balconies, three entrances, one gate,
one terrace, and a garden of citrus trees, the palazzo
presented endless opportunities for Marie to cast her
transformational bohemian spell. But before she could
dive into decorating, her husband John, the pragmatist
in the partnership and a veteran of many ambitious yet
successful renovation projects, had to get to grips with
repairing the ancient structure: a leaking roof, limewashed

**A sensitive but adventurous designer, Marie
has kept much of the original patina. This is
what you buy a palazzo for, after all** (right). **She
has a magpie's eye for ersatz vintage pieces,
which she employs to great effect** (opposite).

Sicily moves to the Savannah
when friend Mirja Ilkka arrives to
paint grisaille murals in a salon. A
Tuareg rug completes the journey.

A typical MO Interiors mash-up combines an oriental wall hanging , an Italian 1970s glass and metal side table and a distressed leather sofa, pieces collected by Marie for her design projects and shipped to Italy to furnish the palazzo (opposite). She was determined to preserve the pigmented walls buried under layers of wallpaper. While many of the floor tiles are original (this page), Marie also introduced some from Marrakech Design.

walls covered in moldy wallpaper, a primitive kitchen, and bleak bathrooms. And all of this work was undertaken with the youngest of the couple's five children tagging along.

As Marie is something of an interiors celebrity in her native Sweden, it was only to be expected that a Swedish TV channel would decide to make a fly-on-the-wall documentary series about the metamorphosis, following the inevitable highs and lows of taking on a large historic building with a scant grasp of Italian, an ever-expanding punch list, and a finite budget. At one point, John earns money building roads in Sweden living out of a caravan, while Marie, in Sicily, is able to tackle more aesthetically satisfying projects, like the addition of monochrome frescoes depicting African wildlife on the walls of the salon, or the installation of her collection of vintage furniture (including those Murano chandeliers) shipped from Sweden

The palazzo showcases Marie's knack for unexpected juxtapositions of old and new, antique and kitsch, rustic and baroque (opposite). Marie specializes in acquiring extraordinary rugs, which she uses for her design projects but also sells. Her signature look, as seen here, relies on layering lots of luscious textures (this page).

and patiently schlepped through the narrow streets by handcart.

Growing up in Hogenas, a small town in the south of Sweden, Marie and her sister were brought up by a single-parent father, a car mechanic by trade. 'I say I was born in a garage,' says Marie, who inherited her father's daydreams of castles, châteaux, and vineyards seen in magazines, and gravitated to anything with a 'past', be it a dress or a dressing table. 'I have always felt like an outsider, rootless, with a hard childhood, so I lived a lot in the imagination,' she explains. A rebellious, challenging teenager, Marie settled down once she found that designing transportive interiors was her ideal creative outlet. 'I set up scenes and I want the picture, the room, the environment to talk to you. You should feel it, like I feel it when I make it.' Although her style, with its glamorous flourishes and baroque kookiness, is quite a departure from

'I SET UP SCENES AND I WANT THE PICTURE, THE ROOM, THE ENVIRONMENT
TO TALK TO YOU. YOU SHOULD FEEL IT, LIKE I FEEL IT WHEN I MAKE IT'

An Italian glass chandelier, a Tuleh rug from Morocco, and a modular leather sofa hold court in the salon (opposite). A vintage painted glass panel in shades of violet and caramel is perfectly in sync with Marie's Biba vibe (above right). She may live in an ancient building, but she always brings some modern lines to the mix (right).

Why not bring mid-century Italian chairs to the Savannah (this page and opposite)**?**

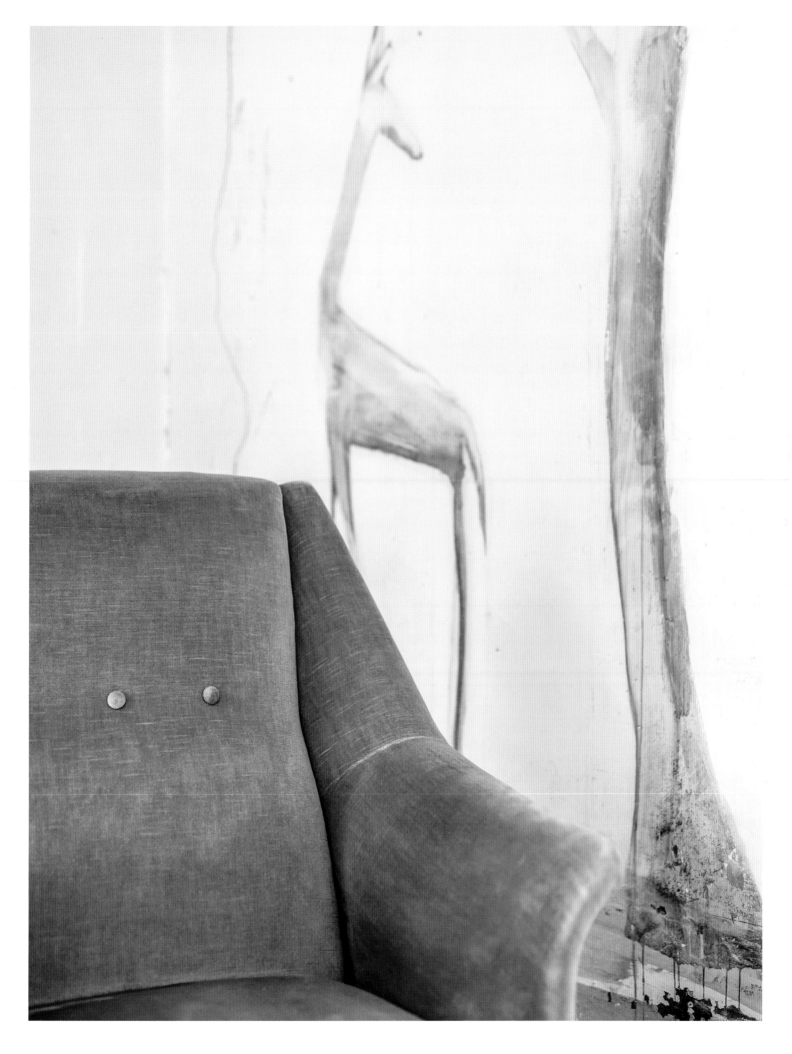

Unexpectedly, for all its expansive living area, the palazzo has a decidedly bijou kitchen; big on charm but short on square meters. Marie's solution? Just add art and a **chandelier** (opposite and this page).

the usual clean-lined Scandinavian tropes, it has found its audience and she is able to earn a living as a wandering scavenger of beauty; pieces she either uses herself, or sells on Instagram or at one of the flea markets staged at her Swedish home.

Like many nomads lucky enough to flit between two cultures, Marie finds that in Sweden she misses Sicily, and vice versa. She values the time spent with family at the palazzo, but has plans to share it with others by offering yoga and creative retreats there. Who knows how the post-pandemic world will affect this kind of enterprise, but rest assured that Marie will find a way to amass more treasures, and satisfy her restless nomadic soul and, by extension, ours too.

Marie and her team were able to preserve the plastered walls, rich with pigment, and the encaustic floor tiles. Nothing else is needed, just sumptuous textiles and a turquoise Berber rug (this page and opposite).

MINIMALISTS IN THE MEDINA

Marrakech's medina, the ancient walled city within the city, is a baffling labyrinth of narrow winding alleyways and shadowy tunnels, a patchwork of crumbling rose-colored plaster facades punctuated by doors. There are no clues. Intriguing, forbidding, dusty, studded, plain, decorative, ancient, gnarled, lacquered in paint or scarred and blistered by the sun, these doorways must be memorized if you ever want to find your way home. They are the portals to other worlds, other stories, the traveler's equivalent to Narnia's improbable wardrobe entrance. Whatever goes on beyond, whatever decorative fantasy attempted and realized, it is impossible to imagine, every riad being exactly as original as its proprietor. Of course, there are the tropes; the *Hideous Kinky* hippy-trail vibe, the saturated pigments, the tile and tadelakt, the jasmine and citrus trees, the soothing trickle of a fountain or cooling courtyard plunge pool, but even so there are always surprises; a design vocabulary for every taste, from monastic to maximalist.

Sarah and Grégoire's take on Moorish minimalism relies on a sophisticated caramel and ivory color palette. Nude leather, weathered wood, and off-white canvas warm up the pale walls and floors of the crisply renovated riad (opposite). Furniture shapes are simple and spare, the accessories primitive and sculptural (above). A bedroom in the gallery is accessed via an ancient style of door within a door (right).

French-Belgians Sarah and Grégoire Rasson's Riad 42 could more easily be defined by what it lacks than what it contains. This is the minimalist's Moorish fantasy, a home reduced to its tactile essentials, without a lick of color or single flourish of pattern, but deeply soulful all the same. 'We think of the architecture as the decoration,' explains Sarah, a Françoise Hardy lookalike who navigates her way around the walled city, a willowy black leather-clad shadow on a black scooter. In my mind hovers that rather bossy diktat 'ornament is crime', but however imperious the Adolf Loos mantra, uncompromising simplicity is convincing here. Minimalism 'fits us', says Sarah. 'We couldn't imagine living any other way.'

Arranged above the central courtyard, the riad's bedrooms are simple elongated rectangles with high, high ceilings and sufficient space for thoughts to drift about uninterrupted by visual distraction. They are

The riad's layout offers multiple seating areas, all set up with a round tea table for the inevitable pots of sweet, hot mint infusions (above). **Worn wooden bowls accessorize at floor level** (above left). **This arrangement is tucked to one side of the gallery, where you will also find the four bedrooms** (opposite). **Soaring ceilings and low furniture enhance the feeling of spaciousness and serenity. Parchment-colored tadelakt floors and detailing are contrasted with the chalky white walls** (opposite and pages 178–179).

THE FAMILY VALUES THE CHANGE OF
RHYTHM THAT THEY FOUND IN MOROCCO,
APPRECIATING A GENTLER PACE AND NEW
SENSE OF FREEDOM

Instead of upper cabinets, the pared-down kitchen has been fitted with tadelakt shelves storing and displaying ceramics and kitchenware. This sealed plaster surface makes an ideal waterproof counter and backsplash. Reclaimed wood doors add another raw, monochromatic texture. This type of kitchen is built as a wooden framework, then the whole plastered with tadelakt (opposite and below left). The *bhou* is an alcove seating area in the ground-floor courtyard (pages 182-183).

perfectly bare but they are also perfectly comforting and comfortable. The crude wooden beds are cozy with anxiety-quelling heavy yak's wool hand-loomed blankets finished with large pompoms (a traditional touch of whimsy), and the internal windows are fitted with wooden shutters but missing glass, encouraging peaceful communication within. Floors are cool, smooth ivory-colored tadelakt softened with monochrome Berber rugs. These mezzanine rooms are accessed via a diminutive cut-out wooden door within a door that a child would enjoy, a traditional design that adds warmth and texture.

Below the courtyard offers communal space; a *bhou* or recessed seating alcove with a long, low bench seat, and a cozier salon hidden behind an unobtrusive glass door. This is the place to retreat to on chilly evenings, to sit by a crackling fire and consume a tagine and couscous with a glass of wine. The rooftop garden, shaded by tented salons with mattresses for lounging on, provides the opportunity to spy on the patchwork of other rooftops belonging to other riads, some so near that you could almost pass the mint teapot between them.

Based in Paris, the Rassons found their pared-down nirvana in 2006 after a trip or two to the city, where they began asking themselves 'what if?', the question that incipient nomads falling under the spell of a new territory are bound to pose. Sarah was originally a nursery school teacher, a career that she notes demanded similar qualities to her new role as chatelaine: patience, calm, equanimity. Grégoire, a graphic designer with a penchant for designing buildings, found his métier running the renovations himself.

Initially their eight-year-old son was not such an easy adaptor, refusing to eat his yoghurt from unfamilar

Light is the most decorative element in this monastic bedroom (left and below). Tactile textures soften the austerity and hanging lights made from woven baskets prevent the room from taking itself too seriously (opposite).

packaging, but more than a decade later, a student of interior design at the Académie Royale des Beaux-Arts in Brussels, he is, according to his mother, a real 'Marrakechi in his heart', always keen to return to his life in the city during vacations. The family values the change of rhythm that they found in Morocco, appreciating a gentler pace and new sense of freedom here. 'We live in organized chaos and we like it like that,' says Sarah.

Since we visited, the Rassons have recently acquired another riad that they are living in and restoring, but future plans include a project in Puglia, Italy where they will no doubt import their particular brand of *luxe, calme, et volupté*; sensual minimalism for modern nomads.

HIRAETH – A LONGING FOR HOME

If you have ever longed for somewhere, an elusive place where you feel you belong but have never found, then you will understand the concept of *hiraeth*. Heather Chontos identified so strongly with the Welsh word when she discovered it that she had it tattooed on her right foot (adding a mysterious circle on the left). In fact, she seems to have led her life according to the demands of that longing, a self-elected nomad propelled toward a destination unknown, wondering where the journey will end.

So far Heather, a single mother of two daughters, has made homes in London, Paris, New York City, Barcelona, Maine, Montana, Berlin, and Bolzano, Italy – perhaps not in that order – with extended stays in New Zealand and Tanzania. Most recently, she has established herself in the tiny hamlet of La Tour-Blanche, Cercles, Nouvelle Aquitaine, France. This latest home, a couple of ancient rustic stone buildings where Heather has been able to combine both family life and her work as an artist, is the first that she has actually owned. She bought it after much online research and sealed the deal without being able to view the property in person, perceiving that it had solid bones and trusting her gut on the rest. She is keen to prove to her daughters, Zanna, 12, and Kodie, 22, that despite inevitable red tape or inconveniences, this freewheeling state is a viable way to live. 'Feel the fear and do it anyway' seems to be her motto, and she hopes that this ad hoc life has instilled a similar fearlessness into the girls.

Heather bought the house sight unseen, but it has proven to be a perfect canvas for her – literally. The stone barn next door to the main house is her atelier and laboratory for sculptural projects (opposite). **The sofa in the main living space is covered in linen designed by Heather for French fabric house Pierre Frey, an abstract explosion of color** (right). **Heather has plans to make the upper floor of the barn atelier into a self-contained apartment** (pages 188–189).

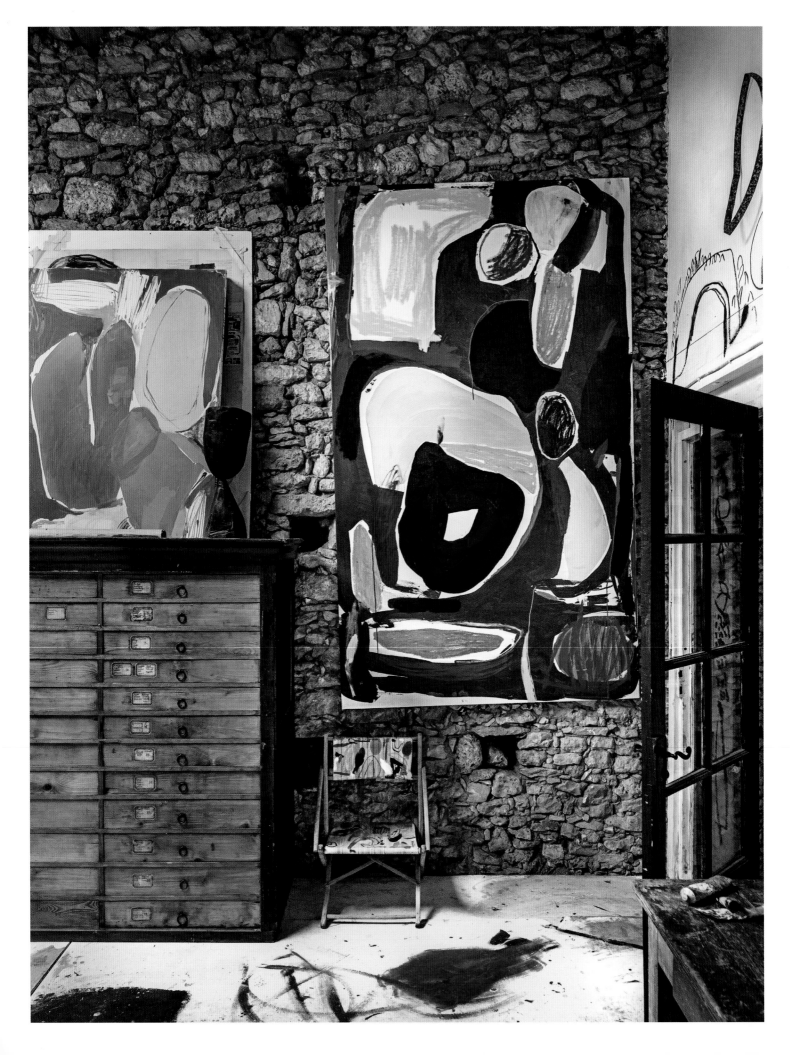

Heather works intuitively on the floor, so naturally it has become another canvas (opposite). A sitting area next door to her studio is furnished with a painted sofa prototype, while the walls are collaged in doodles, scraps, ideas, and ephemera. Arriving with nothing meant being inventive with items found at the local '*dépôt-vente*' (below and right).

The most recent chapter started in Bolzano, Italy where Heather was making a temporary stop to regroup after moving from a two-year stint in Berlin. Ironically, just as she was about to put down new roots in France, the impending COVID-19 situation added complications to her move; that and the fact that she fell in love there with Italian Luis. After Zanna decided to head to New York to stay with her father instead of moving to France, the couple navigated the journey from Italy to Austria, then Switzerland. Here, Luis scratched the 'I' for Italy off the car number plate, worried that coming from Italy would make it tricky to cross the last border into France.

As a serial homemaker Heather is adept at improvisation, her make-do-and-mend attitude to decorating resulting in a gloriously individual space where rules don't apply. 'You've Heathered it,' said

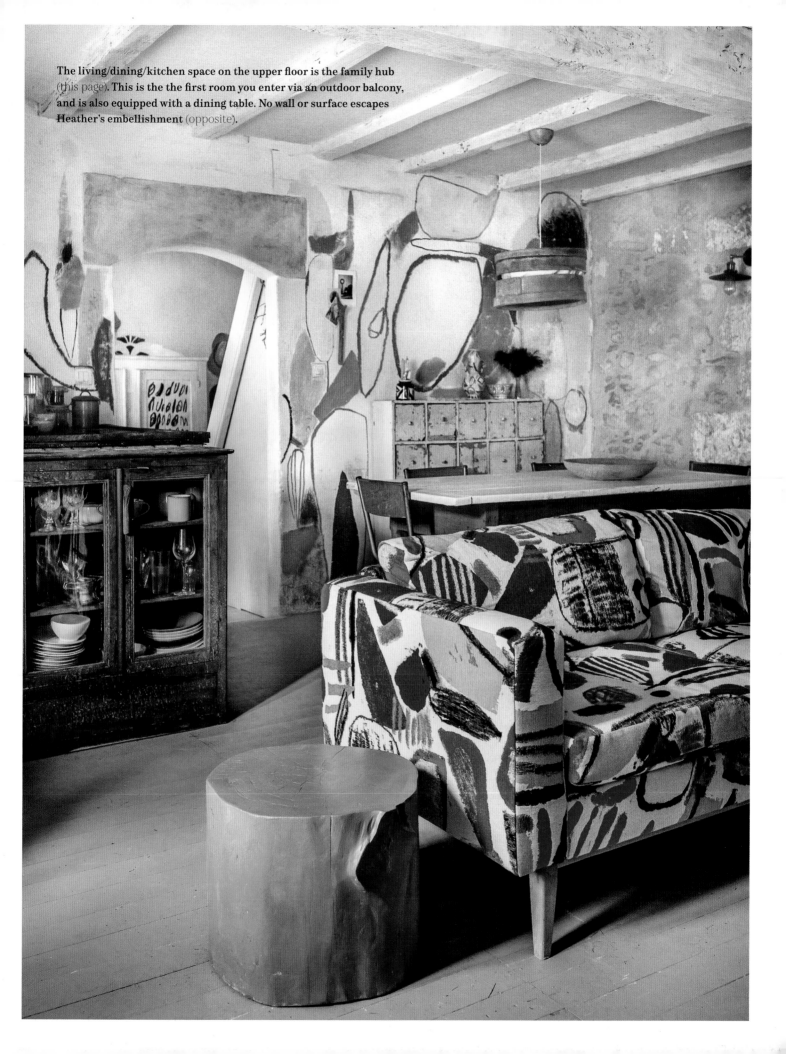

The living/dining/kitchen space on the upper floor is the family hub
(this page). This is the the first room you enter via an outdoor balcony,
and is also equipped with a dining table. No wall or surface escapes
Heather's embellishment (opposite).

daughter Zanna on seeing her new home when she finally made it to join her mother in France after the extended visit to her father and grandparents in New York, lengthened by a tricky year of COVID travel restrictions. Her term nails Heather's resourceful decorating style, where no surface escapes her signature biomorphic shapes: scratches and splashes in gorgeous saturated shades of scarlet, pink, ocher, and indigo. Even the furniture has been improved with paint and her favorite oil sticks; particularly striking is an armoire painted a flat pale gray and applied with Cy Twombly-style scribbles.

Due to the pandemic, when Heather moved here she wasn't able to shop for furniture or art materials or even to wander further than 9½ miles/15km from home. Ever resourceful, she made friends with the owners of Ali Baba, the local vide-grenier, full of things gleaned from house clearances. Here she found old books, maps, and stiff vintage linen, which she employed as an alternative to paper, painting with her own concoction of children's gouache and acrylics from the local supermarket mixed with house paint. She named the series of works that emerged from this period 'Vulnerability', a state with which she has certainly come to terms in the past two years, but from her

Sculptures that echo the amorphous shapes of Heather's paintings were made from pieces of charred wood or rubbed with intensely colored pigment (opposite). The upcycled monochrome cabinet is decorated with Twombly-like scribbles (above). Heather has made the found vessels her own by adding signature shapes and lines.

The upstairs hallway doubles as an office (this page), up to which the stairs have banisters fashioned from driftwood and a web of string, and where a ladder doubles as a bookcase. The steep yellow staircase leads to an attic bedroom (opposite).

A low-ceilinged attic bedroom divided by beams requires some athleticism from the occupant, but every dog has his day. Textiles by Heather, of course (opposite). **Birch wood found in a German forest when Heather was living in Berlin became a series of charred sculptures** (this page).

nomadic CV one suspects is her preferred modus operandi. Every move demands an openness to change, a propensity for adaptation, speaking other languages, and forging new connections.

Turning the buildings she had bought into a viable home required no small amount of physical labor. The garden and barn were full of rubbish that had to be cleared, walls needed insulation, open spaces were divided with recycled doors, and windows, and precarious wooden stairways were added. Currently the two unconnected stone buildings serve as studio and home. On the 'home' side, Heather made a new kitchen improvised from pallets and reclaimed wood, which is part of an open-plan living area. Downstairs she added a bathroom and made a second bedroom for Zanna. Future plans include creating a self-contained apartment connected to her atelier, which has its own garden entrance.

Now due to her industriousness, the 'potager' garden explodes with an enviable amount of produce; orange pumpkins tumble across pathways (unable to operate within the lines, rather like the resident gardener), grapevines clamber up fences, and a jungle of heavy-headed sunflowers, nasturtiums, kale, and salad greens are all available for Heather and Luis, a chef, to plunder for meals eaten on the balcony.

Ask if this is *the* place and she might fudge an answer. For such a talented and energetic creator of worlds, perhaps the 'place' was always with her; it is Heather's will that manifests it and evidently that ability will always be hers wherever she goes.

The kitchen is a masterclass in repurposing with enormous charm. The sink is a zinc bucket, the waste hidden with a length of vintage linen slung loosely over a weathered stick. Necessity is the mother of invention – and, in Heather's home, beauty (this page and opposite).

SOURCES

THE NOMADS

Riad Dar K
– featured in the introduction
www.riad-dar-k.com
IG: @riad_dar_k
Thanks to Riad Dar K in Marrakech for our stay.

Anywhere but Here
– Hilary Robertson, Alistair and Gus McCowan
www.hilaryrobertson.com
IG: @hilaryrobertson

The Schoolhouse
www.locationdepartment.net/locations/3070
IG: @theschoolhousect
Schoolhouse in New England.

Agnès in Wonderland
– Agnès Emery
IG: @agnes.emery

Emery & Cie
www.emeryetcie.com
Paint, tiles, furniture, wallpaper, and ceramics.

No Place like Rome
– Liselotte Watkins
www.worldofwatkins.com
IG: @liselottewatkins
Fine art and illustration.

Less is Moore
– September and Colin Moore
IG: @septembermooreprojects
Interior design.

Nomadsland
– Riad Baoussala
www.baoussala.com
IG: @riadbaoussala

Medina in Monochrome
– Valérie Barkowski
www.valeriebarkowski.shop
IG: @valeriebarkowski
Designer of linens for table, bath and bedroom.

Dar Kawa
www.darkawa.net
IG: @darkawa_riad
Valérie's riad in Marrakech.

Desert Hearts
– Denise Portmans
www.merchantmodern.com
IG: @merchantmodern
Art, furniture, rugs, and ceramics.

Merchant House High Desert
merchantmodern@gmail.com
IG: @merchanthousehighdesert
Rent the desert retreat or the Airstream in Joshua Tree.

Rock the Kasbah
– Marie Olsson Nylander
IG: @marieolssonnylander

MO Interior
www.mointerior.com
@vintage.mo
Interiors stylist with a website of curated vintage finds for sale.

Minimalists in the Medina
– Sarah and Grégoire Rasson

Riad 42
theriad42@gmail.com
IG:@riad42marrakech

Hiraeth – A Longing for Home – Heather Chontos
www.heatherchontos.com
IG: @heatherjchontos
Artist, painter and sculptor.

Tourrette
tourretteparis.com
IG: @tourrette_paris
Heather's gallery in Paris

MATERIALS

Ancient & Modern
www.ancientandmodern.us
IG: @ancientandmodernus
Fireplaces, furniture and staircases in stone and marble.

Bauwerk Colour
www.bauwerkcolour.com
IG: @bauwerkcolour
Pre-mixed lime paint.

Boston Ornament Company
www.bostonornament.com
IG: @bostonornamentco
Tadelakt application.

Clé
www.cletile.com
IG: @cletile
Tiles in a variety of materials.

Kalklitir
www.kalklitir.com
IG: @kalklitir
VOC-free lime paint in powder form.

Portola Paints & Glazes
www.portolapaints.com
IG: @portolapaints
Pre-mixed lime paint and Roman clay plaster.

NOMAD STYLE

Aeand
www.aeand.com
IG: @aeandstudio
Printed textiles and art.

Beck & Cap
www.beckandcap.com
IG: @beckandcap
Chainsaw chairs and organic modern wooden furniture.

Bloomist
www.bloomist.com
IG: @mybloomist
Dried botanicals, vases, and décor.

Caravane
www.caravane.fr
IG: @caravane_paris
Interiors brand with stores in France, London, and San Francisco.

Chama Rugs
www.chamarugs.com
IG: @chamarugs
Handmade Berber rugs.

Clic
www.clic.com
IG: @clic_usa
Art and home décor.

Coquo
www.coquo.ca
IG: @coquo_mtl
Custom modular kitchens from a firm based in Montreal, Canada.

Couleur Locale
www.couleurlocale.eu
IG: @couleurlocaleconceptstore
Global interiors and crafts.

Etsy
www.etsy.com
IG: @etsy
An online marketplace for independent designer-makers, vintage furniture, and accessories.

Graham and Green
www.grahamandgreen.co.uk
IG: @grahamandgreen
Furniture and accessories with an international feel.

HK Living
www.hklivingusa.com
www.hkliving.com (Europe)
IG: @hklivingusa
International brand offering furniture, lighting, and accessories.

Intiearth
www.intiearth.com
IG: @intiearth
Traditional Peruvian frazadas, pillows and baskets.

La Métairie de Montgeard
www.lametairiedemontgeard.fr
IG: @lametairiedemontgeard
Interiors and lifestyle store in a French village near Toulouse.

LRNCE
www.lrnce.com
IG: @lrnce
Design studio based in Marrakech producing textiles, ceramics, and rugs.

Menu Space
www.menuspace.com
IG: @menuspace
Contemporary Scandinavian furniture, lighting, and accessories.

Merci
www.merci-merci.com
IG: @merciparis
Linens, furniture, home accessories, and tableware.

Skagerak
www.skagerak.com
IG: @skagerak
Danish furniture and homeware.

Sunbrella
www.sunbrella.com
IG: @sunbrella
Water-resistant performance fabrics for outdoor use.

Super Marché
www.sfgirlbybay.com/shop
IG: @shopsupermarche
French vintage homeware curated by Californian blogger SF Girl by Bay.

Tine K Home
www.tinekhome.com
IG: @tinekhomeofficial
Bohemian living, indoor and outdoor furniture, and accessories.

Two Dawson
www.two-dawson.com
IG: @twodawson
Comfortable linen bedding.

PHOTOGRAPHY CREDITS

Key: Ph = photographer; a = above; b = below; l = left; c = centre; r = right.

All photography © Ryland Peters & Small 2022 unless otherwise stated.

1 Ph Hilary Robertson/The home of architect and designer Agnès Emery in Marrakech www.emeryetcie.com; 2 Ph Anna Malmberg/The home of artist Heather Chontos in France www.heatherchontos.com; 4–5 Ph Mike Karlsson Lundgren/Riad Baoussala in Essaouira owned by Dominique Choupin and decorated by Léah Bonnet of Bohême of Morocco www.baoussala.com; 6 Ph Hilary Robertson; 8 Ph Mike Karlsson Lundgren/The home of architect and designer Agnès Emery in Marrakech www.emeryetcie.com; 11 Ph Mike Karlsson Lundgren 12 Ph © Anna Malmberg/Proyecto Público Prim in Mexico City www.proyectopublicoprim.com; 14 Ph © Laurie Frankel; 15 Ph © Anna Malmberg/Proyecto Público Prim in Mexico City www.proyectopublicoprim.com; 16 Ph Mike Karlsson Lundgren/Riad Baoussala in Essaouira owned by Dominique Choupin and decorated by Léah Bonnet of Bohême of Morocco www.baoussala.com; 18–19 Ph © Mike Karlsson Lundgren; 20 Ph Mike Karlsson Lundgren/Riad Dar K in Marrakech owned by Sibel and Valentin Bentz www.riad-dar-k.com; 21 al Ph © Mike Karlsson Lundgren; 21 all other photographs Ph Mike Karlsson Lundgren/Riad Dar K in Marrakech owned by Sibel and Valentin Bentz www.riad-dar-k.com; 22 Ph © Dana Gallagher/The Schoolhouse in Connecticut owned by author and interior designer Hilary Robertson www.hilaryrobertson.com; 23 Ph © Anna Malmberg/The home of photographer Anna Malmberg; 24–27 Ph © Dana Gallagher/The Schoolhouse in Connecticut owned by author and interior designer Hilary Robertson www.hilaryrobertson.com; 28–29 Ph Frank Frances/Merchant House High Desert in California, the home of interior designer and store owner Denise Portmans of Merchant www.merchantmodern.com; 30 Ph Mike Karlsson Lundgren; 31 Ph Mike Karlsson Lundgren/The home of architect and designer Agnès Emery in Marrakech www.emeryetcie.com; 32 Ph Mike Karlsson Lundgren/Riad Dar K in Marrakech owned by Sibel and Valentin Bentz www.riad-dar-k.com; 34–35 Ph Mike Karlsson Lundgren/Riad 42 in Marrakech owned by Sarah and Grégoire Rasson www.instagram.com/riad42marrakech; 36–37 Ph Frank Frances/Merchant House High Desert in California, the home of interior designer and store owner Denise Portmans of Merchant www.merchantmodern.com; 38 Ph Mike Karlsson Lundgren; 40 Ph © Dana Gallagher; 41 Ph Frank Frances/Merchant House High Desert in California, the home of interior designer and store owner Denise Portmans of Merchant www.merchantmodern.com; 42 Ph © Mike Karlsson Lundgren; 43 Ph © Mike Karlsson Lundgren; 44–45 Ph Mike Karlsson Lundgren; 46 Ph Mike Karlsson Lundgren/The home of architect and designer Agnès Emery in Marrakech www.emeryetcie.com; 47 Ph Mike Karlsson Lundgren; 48 Ph © Dana Gallagher/The Schoolhouse in Connecticut owned by author and interior designer Hilary Robertson www.hilaryrobertson.com; 50–51 Ph © Laurie Frankel/usage courtesy of Sunbrella/Glen Raven; 52–53 Ph © Kate Mathis/ The Schoolhouse in Connecticut owned by author and interior designer Hilary Robertson www.hilaryrobertson.com; 54 Ph Mike Karlsson Lundgren/Riad Dar K in Marrakech owned by Sibel and Valentin Bentz www.riad-dar-k.com; 56–71 Ph Dana Gallagher/The Schoolhouse in Connecticut owned by author and interior designer Hilary Robertson www.hilaryrobertson.com; 72–83 Ph Mike Karlsson Lundgren/The home of architect and designer Agnès Emery in Marrakech www.emeryetcie.com; 84–97 Ph Mike Karlsson Lundgren/The home of artist Liselotte Watkins in Rome www.worldofwatkins.com; 98–111 Ph Anna Malmberg/The home of interior designer September Moore in France www.instagram.com/septembermooreprojects; 112–125 Ph Mike Karlsson Lundgren/Riad Baoussala in Essaouira owned by Dominique Choupin and decorated by Léah Bonnet of Bohême of Morocco www.baoussala.com; 126–141 Ph Mike Karlsson Lundgren/Riad Dar Kawa in Marrakech owned by creative director Valérie Barkowski www.darkawa.net www.valeriebarkowski.com; 142–157 Ph Frank Frances/Merchant House High Desert in California, the home of interior designer and store owner Denise Portmans of Merchant www.merchantmodern.com; 158–173 Ph Mike Karlsson Lundgren/Palazzo Cirillo in Sicily owned by Marie Olsson Nylander of MO Interior www.mointerior.com; 174–185 Ph Mike Karlsson Lundgren/Riad 42 in Marrakech owned by Sarah and Grégoire Rasson www.instagram.com/riad42marrakech; 186–201 Ph Anna Malmberg/The home of artist Heather Chontos in France www.heatherchontos.com; 206–207 Ph © Dana Gallagher/The Schoolhouse in Connecticut owned by author and interior designer Hilary Robertson www.hilaryrobertson.com.

INDEX

Page numbers in *italic* refer to the illustrations

A
Académie Royale des Beaux-Arts, Brussels 184
Adam Ant 13
adobe 27
Airbnb 19, 51
Ali Baba, Cercles 195
Allen, Woody 58
Amangiri, Utah desert 13
Amsterdam 9, 57
Annaleena 42
Arles 13
Ashley, Laura 9
The Audo, Copenhagen 14
Austria 191

B
balconies 34, *72–3*, *111*
bamboo furniture 34
Baoussala, Essaouira *46–7*, *112–25*, *113–23*
Barcelona 187
Barkowski, Valérie 34, *126–41*, *127–37*
Barneys, New York City 85–6
Baron, Languedoc 108
baskets *40*
bathrooms: Agnès Emery's house, Marrakech *75*
    Connecticut schoolhouse *64*, 71, *71*
    Dar Kawa, Marrakech 132
    Languedoc *chambre d'hôte* *111*
Bauwerk Colour 98, 107, 108–11
bedrooms: Agnès Emery's house, Marrakech *76–7*
    Baoussala, Essaouira *122*
    Connecticut schoolhouse *68*, 71
    Dar Kawa, Marrakech 132, *132–3*, *140–1*
    La Tour-Blanche, Cercles *198*, 199
    Languedoc *chambre d'hôte* *104–7*, 111
    Palazzo Cirillo, Sicily *172–3*
    Riad 42, Marrakech *175*, *176–81*, *184–5*
    Rome apartment *96–7*
beds, four-poster 19, *20*
Belgium 27
Berber Lodge 25

Berbers 10, 114, 181
Berlin 187, 191
Bertoia 132
Biba 159, 167
Birger, Malene *42*
Bloomist 58
Bloomsbury Group 71
Bolzano 187, 191
boutique hotels 19
BOY 13
Brooklyn 13
Brutalism 13, 14, *18*
Byron, Lord 13

C
California 33
Camellas Lloret, Languedoc *98–111*, *99–111*
Carcassonne 108
Casa Cook, Mykonos, Greece 19, *25*
casein (milk) paint 27, 76
ceramics *28–9*
Cercles, Nouvelle Aquitaine *186–201*, *187–99*
Cézanne, Paul 108
@charlottetyl 14
Chelsea Hotel, New York City 85
Chiang Mai 127
Chontos, Heather *186–201*, *187–99*
Cocteau, Jean 13
colour 38, 39–42, *40–7*
Connecticut schoolhouse *57–71*, *65–71*
Copenhagen 9, 14
Coquo 68
courtyards: Agnès Emery's house, Marrakech *72–3*
    Dar Kawa, Marrakech *126*, 127
    Mexico *12*, *15*
    Riad 42, Marrakech *181*, *182–3*
COVID-19 pandemic 191, 195
Cubism 85, 90

D
Dar K, Marrakech *20–1*, *32*, *54*
Dar Kawa, Marrakech 34, *126–41*, *127–37*
daybeds *56*
Denmark 9, 57
Design Nomad 10
dining rooms: Baoussala,

Essaouira *112*, *114*
    Dar Kawa, Marrakech *129*
    La Tour-Blanche, Cercles *192–3*, *199*
    Languedoc *chambre d'hôte* *100–2*, *111*
    Palazzo Cirillo, Sicily *164*
    Rome apartment *84–6*, *89*, *90*, *94*
doors *130*, *175*, *181*

E
El Fenn, Marrakech 17, 127
Emery, Agnès 8, *30–1*, 34, *46–7*, *72–83*, *73–8*
encaustic tiles *30–1*, *75*, *80–1*, *172–3*
entrance halls *86*, *94*
Essaouira *112–25*, *113–23*
Etsy 39

F
Fiat 159
floating furniture *56*
floor materials *25*
Fornasetti *89*
four-poster beds 19, *20*
France 9, 51
    La Tour-Blanche, Cercles *186–201*, *187–99*
    Languedoc *chambre d'hôte* *98–111*, *99–111*

G
Gainey, Ryan 102
Gallipoli, Puglia *50–1*
Germany 9
Greece 19, 25, 42

H
Hannah, Sophie 17
Hermès 86
HIP Hotels 19
Ho Chi Minh City 127
Hogenas, Sweden 167
Hotel Menorca Experimental 19
hotels 14, 17–19, *20–1*

I
Ilkka, Mirja *160–1*
India 40
Instagram 14, 39, 99
Into the Garden, Tampa, Florida 102–8
Ireland 39
Italy 102, 184, 187, 191

Palazzo Cirillo, Sicily *158–73*, *159–71*
Rome apartment *84–97*, *86–95*

J
Jack Rabbit Studio 70
Jackson, Atlanta 102
Janowitz, Tana 58
Jutland 9

K
Kalman, Maira 58
kitchens: Agnès Emery's house, Marrakech *78*, *80–1*
    Baoussala, Essaouira *115*
    Connecticut schoolhouse *65*, 68
    Dar Kawa, Marrakech *134–5*
    La Tour-Blanche, Cercles 199, *200–1*
    Languedoc *chambre d'hôte* *110–11*, *111*
    outdoor kitchens 36, *36–7*
    Palazzo Cirillo, Sicily *170–1*
    Riad 42, Marrakech *180–1*
    Rome apartment *88–9*, *90–5*

L
La DoubleJ 90
La Tour-Blanche, Cercles, Nouvelle Aquitaine *186–201*, *187–99*
Languedoc *chambre d'hôte* *98–111*, *99–111*
lava stone 24
León, John 63
Lewis, Rick 58
light, and color 42
lime plaster 27
limestone 24, *26*
limewash/lime paint *12*, 24, 25, 27, 98, 111
Lisbon 49
living rooms: Agnès Emery's house, Marrakech *78–9*
    Baoussala, Essaouira *113*, *116–17*, *120–2*
    Dar Kawa, Marrakech *131*
    La Tour-Blanche, Cercles *192–3*
    Languedoc *chambre d'hôte* 98, *102–3*, 111
    Palazzo Cirillo, Sicily *165–6*, *168–9*
    Riad 42, Marrakech *177*

Rome apartment 90, *91–3*
loggias *14*
London 187
Loos, Adolf 176
Los Angeles 33

M
McCowan, Alistair 71
Maine 39, 187
@maison_de_sable *14*
Mallorca 10
Malmö 10
marble *24*, 25, *26*
markets 39
Marrakech 10, *11*, 17, 40, 113
   Agnès Emery's house *8*,
    30–1, *72–83*, *73–8*
   Dar K *20–1*, *32*, *54*
   Dar Kawa 34, *126–41*,
    127–37
   Riad 42 *34–5*, *174–85*,
    175–84
   rugs *44–5*
Marrakech Design *162*
Masseria Potenti, Puglia 19, *51*
materials *24*, 25–7, *26–32*
Mayle, Peter, *A Year in Provence*
   10
Meilichzon, Dorothée 19
Menorca 19
Merchant House, Morongo
   Valley, California *142–57*,
   143–55
Mexico *12*, *13*, 34, 39, 40
Mexico City 10
Milan 86, 102
milk (casein) paint 27, *76*
Millesgården gallery, Sweden
   90
minimalism 99, 176
mirror tiles *75*, *78*
Montana 187
Montpellier 108
Montréal, Languedoc 108
mood boards *24*, *48*
Moore, Colin 99, 102, 111
Moore, September *98–111*,
   99–111
Morandi, Giorgio 108
Morocco 10, 40, 108
   Baoussala, Essaouira *46–7*,
    112–25, *113–23*
   Agnès Emery's house,
    Marrakech *8*, *30–1*, *72–83*,
    73–8
   Dar K, Marrakech *20–1*, *32*,
    54

Dar Kawa, Marrakech 34,
   126–41, *127–37*
Riad 42, Marrakech *34–5*,
   174–85, *175–84*
   rugs *44–5*
Morongo Valley, California 33,
   41, *142–57*, *143–55*
Morseta, Portugal 17
Morten, Lucas *18–19*
Morton, Meg 40
Murano chandeliers 163, *166*
Mykonos, Greece 25

N
Netherlands 57
New Mexico 27
New Romantics 13
New York City 57–65, 85, 127,
   187, 191
The New York Times 86
New Zealand 187
Nord-Pinus, Arles 13
Norfolk 57
North Africa 38, 42
NYC flower market *51*
Nylander, Marie Olsson
   158–73, *159–71*

O
offices *108–9*, 111, *196–7*
orangery, Connecticut
   schoolhouse *66–9*, 71
Oudolf, Piet 71
outdoor spaces *16*, *32*, *34–5*
   Baoussala, Essaouira *118–19*,
    124–5
   furniture 34
   kitchens 36, *36–7*
   see also balconies; courtyards;
    rooftop spaces

P
paint: limewash/lime paint *12*,
   25, 27, *98*, 111
   milk (casein) paint 27, *76*
Palazzo Cirillo, Sicily *158–73*,
   159–71
Paradero, Todos Santos,
   Mexico 13
Paris 9, 40, 86, 102, 123, 181,
   187
Peru *40*
Picasso, Pablo 13
Pierre Frey 187
Pinterest 10, 68
Pittsburgh 10
plaster 25

lime plaster 27
tadelakt *20–1*, 27, 113, *113*,
   128, *132*, *134*, *177–81*
Portmans, Denise 19, 28, 33,
   36, *41*, *142–57*, *143–55*
Portugal 13, 17
Provence 10
Pueblo architecture 27
Puglia *14*, 19, *50–1*, 184

R
Rasson, Sarah and Grégoire
   174–85, *175–84*
Raynor, Stephane 13
Riad 42, Marrakech *34–5*,
   174–85, *175–84*
Riedel, Bronwyn 107, *108–11*
Roman clay 25, 27
Rome apartment *84–97*, *86–95*
rooftop spaces 10
   Agnès Emery's house,
    Marrakech *8*, *78*, *82–3*
   Baoussala, Essaouira *124–5*
   Dar K, Marrakech *32*
   Dar Kawa, Marrakech 34, *127*
   Riad 42, Marrakech *181*
The Rooster, Greece 19
rugs *44–5*, *160–1*, *164*, *166*
Russia 128

S
Saarinen, Eero *120–1*
San Giorgio hotel, Mykonos,
   Greece 25
Santa Clara 1728, Portugal 17
Santa Fe, New Mexico 27
Scandinavia 9, 42, 57
Schlegel, Valentine 19, 42
Secret Souk hotels, Morocco
   127
serpentine stone *26*
shower rooms 111, *111*
Sicily *158–73*, *159–71*
Siena 95
sitting rooms *see* living rooms
Slowood Studios *14*
SoHo, New York 40
Soho House group *14*
South Africa 102
Spain 111
Stevenson, Robert Louis 10
stone floors 25
studios *188–91*
Sublime Comporta, Portugal
   13
Sunbrella fabrics *51*
Sweden 9, *18–19*, 85, 86, 95,

163, 167, 171
swimming pools 71, *112*
Switzerland 191

T
tadelakt plaster *20–1*, 27, 113,
   113, *128*, *132*, *134*, *177–81*
Tampa, Florida *102–8*
Tanzania 187
Taos, New Mexico 27
Taylor, Lindsey 71
terracotta tiles *99*
Texas 85
tiles: encaustic tiles *30–1*, *75*,
   172–3
   floors 25
   mirror tiles *75*, *78*
   terracotta tiles *99*
   zellige tiles *75*, *132*
Todos Santos, Mexico 13
Tokyo 40
Tuareg rugs *160–1*
Tuleh rugs *166*
Tunisia 42, *52–3*, 58
Tuscany 95
Twist The World 128, *132–7*,
   140–1
Twombly, Cy 195

U
United States of America 102
   Connecticut schoolhouse
    57–71, *65–71*
   Merchant House *142–57*,
    143–55
Utah desert 13
Uzès 108

V
Vaquette, Pascale *28–9*
vernacular architecture 25
Vervoordt, Axel 27
views *33–7*
@visualpleasuretravel *14*
Vreeland, Diana 65

W
wabi-sabi 27, *43*, 113, *143*
Watkins, Liselotte *84–97*,
   85–95
wooden floors 25

Y
Ypma, Herbert 19

Z
zellige tiles *75*, *80–1*, *132*

eva hesse gouaches 1960–1961 Renos Xippas/Robert Miller

HEIZNER   Objects of Desire   POTTER

Emmet Gowin Photographs   Bulfinch

NEW SEASON, NEW MOOD

ACKNOWLEDGMENTS

HILARY TRAVELING HOPEFULLY...

Usually my books start with my own questions about how to live. Before writing this one I thought that, perhaps, if I cross questioned some people who have managed to create a nomadic or peripatetic lifestyle, I might learn how to find my own nirvana. I have loved hearing all their stories (which are as much about designing a fulfilling life and finding your place in the world as they are about a particular style). Thanks to my inspiring 'nomads' for allowing us to observe and capture their homes, for feeding us, and for giving us all those local tips essential to any successful trip.

It turned out that 2019 was a strange year to be producing a book about travel and design and it has taken much longer than planned and more people than I originally imagined to make it. Many thanks to Dana Gallagher who shot my house, Frank Frances and Olivia Demetros who came with me to the Morongo Valley, CA, Anna Malmberg who met me in France to shoot the homes of September Moore and Heather Chontos, and Mike Karlsson Lundgren, who would have shot the entire book had it not been for a pandemic – it was fun while it lasted!

I will be sad not to be in very regular correspondence with my fabulous pen pal – ahem, editor – Annabel Morgan, who writes the most amusing newsy emails about many things other than deadlines, Leslie Harrington who is always the calmest, most understanding creative director, and Paul Tilby, our designer who even thinks of great titles (such as No Place like Rome) and is very tolerant of my endless tweaks. And a big thank you to my pal and sometime boss Leanne Ford for her foreword. Her cheerleading was vital fuel for the mighty task of making another book.

To my #candohusband, Alistair, I promise to stop demanding maid service. I might even start cooking again.